D0789415

# Automating Media Centers and Small Libraries

# Automating Media Centers and Small Libraries

## A Microcomputer-Based Approach

**Second Edition**

**Dania Bilal**
Assistant Professor
School of Information Sciences
The University of Tennessee-Knoxville

2002
Libraries Unlimited
A Division of Greenwood Publishing Group, Inc.
Greenwood Village, Colorado

LIBRARIES UNLIMITED
A Division of Greenwood Publishing Group, Inc.
P.O. Box 6633
Englewood, CO 80155-6633
1-800-237-6124
www.lu.com

**Library of Congress Cataloging-in-Publication Data**

Bilal, Dania, 1956-
    Automating media centers and small libraries : a
microcomputer-based approach / Dania Bilal.-- 2nd ed.
        p. cm.
    Includes bibliographical references and index.
    ISBN 1-56308-879-7 (pbk.)
    1. Small libraries--United States--Automation. 2. School
libraries--United States--Automation. 3. Instructional materials
centers--United States--Automation. I. Title.

Z678.93.S6 B55 2002
025'.00285--dc21

                                              2001050744

*I dedicate this book to my loving father, Mustafa,
and mother, Yusra, whose encouragement and support
have resulted in the writing of this book.
To my sisters, brothers, nephews, and nieces.
To my friends who reside in the United States
and overseas.*

# Contents

# Figures

# Tables

# Foreword

Dania Bilal's first edition of *Automating Media Centers and Small Libraries*: *A Microcomputer-Based Approach* guided thousands of media specialists and librarians as they met the challenge of planning for and installing online public access catalogs, circulation systems, and networks in their libraries. Her new work, a welcome update, once again provides a solid knowledge base for practitioners and students of library and information science. This knowledge is essential as automated systems are rapidly growing more sophisticated and revolutionizing library services.

Several significant developments that occurred after the first edition appeared in 1997 are reflected in the second edition. The Internet has expanded dramatically, influencing several steps in the automation process. Bilal discusses this influence on system selection, retrospective conversion, and system implementation. She provides a clear-cut analysis of using MARC records from the Web from both fee-based and free services. When addressing how OPACs on the Web have now become commonplace, she updates us on advances such as linkages to other libraries, statewide databases, access from home, the 856 field, and integration with reference databases. The impact of the Internet is also evident from the inclusion of Web sites in the reference list at the end of each chapter.

A key new chapter is Chapter 8, on system migration. As the number of school library media centers and libraries with automated systems continues to multiply, countless professionals will face the task of upgrading their existing systems or moving to a new vendor for various reasons. Many might believe this to be an effortless undertaking, but as Bilal points out, numerous time-consuming tasks must be performed. One of the most critical is that of data migration, which is covered in depth.

The Telecommunications Act of 1996 was in its infancy prior to Bilal's first edition. An important component of the act is that libraries and schools applying for discounts must have a technology plan in place. This volume will provide assistance in this area, with its exhaustive attention to the planning process. Wireless networks and client/server architecture, new components discussed, could figure into current technology plans for the library and beyond its walls.

*Information Power: Building Partnerships for Learning*, released in 1998, prescribed more roles and responsibilities for media specialists. My own research demonstrated that automated systems in media centers could free up the media specialist to spend more time in roles deemed important in *Information Power*. Throughout this book, Bilal examines staff time expenditures in planning, preparing, and implementing automated systems and considers staff time to be an integral part of the decision-making process. Automated systems are also viewed within the context of the updated training that is necessary for students to support *Information Power's* nine information literacy standards for student learning.

As they were in the previous edition, readers are guided in a highly readable style through an overview of automated systems, preparing for automation, system architecture and hardware configurations, preparing the collection for the automated system, implementing the automated system, networking, OPACs and the World Wide Web, and future OPACs. Extensive charts, lists, and illustrations add to the clarity of the explanations. Each chapter also includes a summary, numerous references, and a relevant activity, making the work useful as a textbook.

Automating will be one of the most expensive and far-reaching decisions you will make as a librarian or media specialist. This book does not prescribe specific automated systems but rather offers an educated, systematic decision-making approach. The text also deals with the human impact of automation decisions on patrons and staff. When discussing these decisions, Bilal delves into areas not commonly addressed in the literature, such as their political, financial, and social ramifications.

Whether you are automating for the first, second, or third time, this unique book provides a solid foundation to those automating media centers and small libraries. By following the process outlined in this work you will avoid costly mistakes and be successful.

Nancy Everhart, Ph.D., Associate Professor
Division of Library and Information Science, St. John's University
Jamaica, New York

# Acknowledgments

I wish to thank Dr. Richard Pollard, Associate Professor of Information Sciences, at the University of Tennessee-Knoxville, for serving as a referee on Chapter 7 and for sharing his expertise in networking. My thanks are also extended to Dr. Nancy Everhart, Associate Professor of Library and Information Science at St. John's University, for writing the foreword. Special thanks are offered to students in IS 582 (Library Automation) for their invaluable comments and suggestions and for testing partial activities provided in the book.

Grateful acknowledgments are extended to library automation vendors, especially Gary W. Kirk, Vice President of The Library Corporation; and Susan Russell, Automation Consultant at Follett Software Company, for their feedback and prompt replies to my inquiries.

# Introduction

Recent developments in information technologies have had a profound impact on library automation. In the last few years, library automation vendors have added enhancements with new cutting-edge technology, developed cross-platform products, expanded client/server capabilities, implemented the Z39.50 standard to both client and server, continued migration from character-based (DOS) software to Windows and Web interfaces, and developed portals to Web resources to empower patrons to personalize their home pages and gain ultimate experience in information retrieval.

Since 1998, the school library marketplace that predominantly uses micro-based automation systems has become the most competitive as new vendors have moved into this sector to increase their customer base. In fact, school libraries have had the largest market share of micro-based systems in the last few years.

Lack of a library automation text that targets school and small libraries and reflects the impact technological developments have had on library automation has led to the writing of this second edition of *Automating Media Centers and Small Libraries.*

## WHAT IS AN AUTOMATED SYSTEM?

An automated system combines both software and hardware. The software consists of a computer program designed to perform various library functions, such as circulation, cataloging, public access, acquisitions, serials control, and interlibrary loan.

The hardware comprises input devices (e.g., keyboard, mouse), output devices (e.g., printer, monitor), a central processing unit (i.e., microprocessor), main storage (i.e., main memory), secondary storage (e.g., zip disks, hard disks), and communications devices (e.g., Integrated Service Digital Network—ISDN—line, T-1 line). Software and hardware must work concurrently and properly to run an automated system.

Software designed for automation can operate on three categories of computers: mainframes, miniframes, and microcomputers. The differences among these computers are in the processing power, disk storage, memory size, number of terminals or computers supported, intended applications, and cost. Mainframes are suitable for large academic, research, and public libraries with millions of titles in their collections and for consortia (a network of libraries). Miniframes are appropriate for medium-sized libraries with collections of more than 300,000 titles. Microcomputers are recommended for all types of small libraries, such as media centers, corporate libraries, medical libraries, and public libraries with smaller collections. Recent developments in technologies have blurred the differences between these types of computers.

# SMALL VERSUS MEDIUM-SIZED
# AND LARGE LIBRARIES

Small libraries differ from medium-sized and large libraries in terms of their collection size, mission, number of patrons served, level of staffing, funding, and the need for software and hardware for automation. Although the general automation process can be applied to most libraries, media centers and small libraries require a special approach. A media center with limited financial resources, for example, may resort to converting library records (i.e., the shelflist) using in-house original cataloging (after installing the automated system) instead of using a CD-ROM database of MARC 21 records; it may import its MARC 21 records from the Web using free-based services; or it may contract with a commercial vendor (e.g., Follett) instead of a bibliographic utility, such as the Online Computer Library Center (OCLC).

The general similarities among small libraries pertain to the low number of professional staff (i.e., one or two people) and limited financial resources. The differences lie in their mission, type of clientele, kinds of services, and collection. The mission of a media center, for example, is to provide information access and service that meet curriculum, educational, and recreational needs of students, teachers, and staff.

A public library's mission is to render access to information and services to all people to meet their educational, informational, recreational, and cultural needs. The mission of a special library (e.g., medical) is to furnish up-to-date research collection and information services that meet the immediate needs of its clientele. Central to these services, for example, is access to online databases (e.g., Medline) available through commercial vendors, such as DIALOG; this service is not provided by many media centers. Additional differences may pertain to priorities for automating library functions. A medical library may rank the automated serials function as one of its top priorities because of the extensive periodical routing performed within the organization. A public library with branches may consider automated acquisitions a high priority because of its centralized material purchasing and processing. A media center may regard the circulation function as the highest priority for automation because of the intensity of routine tasks involved and the heavy demand for the service. Regardless of the priorities for automation, however, all small libraries may find microcomputer-based integrated automated systems appealing. This is due to the development of integrated software (software with modules that share a common database) with enhanced capabilities that are reasonably priced and designed to suit the needs of various types of small libraries. The Windows-based Circ/Cat Plus from Follett Software Company and the Winnebago Spectrum from Sagebrush Corporation, for example, are suitable for media centers and public libraries. Inmagic, from Inmagic, Inc., is appropriate for special libraries.

# GOALS OF THIS BOOK

This work serves as a textbook for graduate students in library automation as well as a guide for practitioners who are involved in an automation project. Educators of library and information science who teach automation will find that this text provides a systematic explanation of the main steps involved in automation, including planning, selecting, implementing, and evaluating an automated system. In addition, this text includes important processes that take place while carrying out these steps, such as preparing the collection for automation and choosing a network topology and architecture. Although systematic, some processes may occur in parallel. For example, one team may be evaluating software packages (selection process) while another team may be weeding the collection (collection preparation process).

This book furnishes the reader with knowledge and understanding of

> the concepts pivotal to automation and networking;
>
> the overall process and steps involved in automation, with emphasis on media centers and small libraries;
>
> the options for hardware configurations and client/server architecture;
>
> the selection process, including preparation of a Request for Proposal (RFP);
>
> collection preparation, retrospective conversion options, and cost analysis for various options;
>
> MARC 21 and other bibliographic standards central to automation;
>
> collection barcoding procedures;
>
> site preparation, software installation and testing, and system maintenance;
>
> staff and user training;
>
> system evaluation and database maintenance;
>
> the type of networks, components, topologies, and architecture of local area networks (LANs);
>
> wireless LANs (WLANs);
>
> the process of migration from one automation system to another;
>
> the process of establishing a presence for a library's OPAC (online public access catalog) on the World Wide Web; and
>
> recent developments in library automation and the future of OPACs.

# CHANGES TO THIS EDITION

The main changes to this edition are in Chapter 3, "System Architecture and Hardware Configurations." It describes differences between hierarchical and client/server architecture. To clarify differences in hardware configuration for automated systems, it divides it into two categories, non-networked and networked, and describes each category. In the networked environment, the chapter explains the advantages and disadvantages of a local area network (LAN) versus the wide area network (WAN) configuration. In addition, it depicts client/server architecture in more detail, compares it to the traditional file server design model, delineates three main types of this architecture (two-tier, three-tier, and thin clients), and provides the benefits and disadvantages of each type.

Another change is found in Chapter 4, "System Selection," which includes a new section about pitfalls to avoid in a *Don't Do* list format and things to remember during the selection process in a *Do* list. The sample Request for Proposal (RFP), which was developed for a character-based automation system (i.e., DOS-based) in the first edition, has been changed to a Windows-based system.

A new section about importing MARC 21 (MARC for the Twenty-First Century) records from fee-based and free-based Web services has been added to Chapter 5, "Preparing the Collection for the Automated System." Advantages and disadvantages of each service are delineated. The section on MARC 21 has replaced the sections on U.S. MARC (United States Machine-Readable Cataloging) and U.S. MARC/MicroLIF Protocols (United States Machine-Readable Cataloging/Microcomputer Library Interchange Format).

Chapter 6, "Implementing the Automated System," has a new section on system maintenance with special reference to environmental care, system backup, and system security. In addition, it includes a new section on evaluation of system use and gives more attention to staff and patron training.

Chapter 7, "Networking," has been expanded to include all types of networks and their topologies, architecture, and protocols. It covers different types of connections in more detail (e.g., telephone connections, ISDN, Digital Subscriber Lines—DSL, T-carrier lines). Wireless LANs are described in more detail.

A new chapter on system migration (Chapter 8) has been added. As many media specialists and information professionals are faced with the challenge of upgrading their existing automated systems from DOS to Windows interface or migrating completely from an existing system to another, they must become aware of the procedures involved in system migration.

Chapter 9, "OPACs and the World Wide Web" (previously Chapter 8), has been revised and expanded. Chapter 10, "Future OPACs" (formerly Chapter 9), not only covers recent developments in library automation but also discusses the most important trends and issues, including the role of information professionals in dealing with these issues.

# ORGANIZATION OF THIS EDITION

This book is divided into ten chapters. Chapter 1 provides a brief overview of the development of automated systems and describes modules and their functions as well as the differences between integrated and stand-alone systems. It covers the different terminology now used to refer to public access catalogs, such as online public access catalogs (OPACs), Web online public access catalogs (Web OPACs), Internet public access catalogs (IPACs), public access catalogs (PACs), and Web public access catalogs (Web PACs). In addition, it covers the benefits and pitfalls of library automation.

Chapter 2 describes how to prepare for automation. Preparing for automation means planning. Planning is an ongoing process that does not end with the implementation of the automated system. This process requires knowledge acquisition or learning about automation; the reader is pointed to a number of resources, including journals, trade shows, and experienced colleagues. Needs assessment involves determining staff needs and preparing them for change, assessing user needs, and appointing an automation advisory committee to coordinate the automation project. Needs assessment also includes analyzing functions and tasks using charts or workflow patterns, as well as gathering quantitative data about each function that will provide a rationale for automation. The chapter offers several lists of items that should be considered before one decides whether or how to automate. This part of the process can be time-consuming, but it is vitally important to understanding how and where the automation system should be used to create the most benefit. The last step in needs assessment is analysis and interpretation of the collected data, which helps one determine priorities for automation. To facilitate needs assessment, the chapter details a step-by-step approach to data gathering, analysis, and interpretation. Finally, Chapter 2 makes the point that automation is not performed to save money. Sources of funding for the automation project should be identified. A cost estimate of the project, including ongoing expenses, should be done at the outset. Items to include in the estimate are discussed. Automation does not save money. Rather, it is carried out to improve media center or library services; enhance access to the collection; and increase productivity, accuracy, and efficiency. The chapter ends with an activity that allows readers to practice various processes involved in needs assessment.

All information professionals, including media specialists, are (or shortly will be) affected by automation to some degree. Therefore, all must be aware of the differences that characterize various automated systems: platform (e.g., Macintosh, IBM-PC compatible systems), operating system (e.g., Windows NT, Unix), the kind of computer system (microcomputers, miniframes, and mainframes), and the type of client/server architecture employed. Chapter 3 briefly describes these differences. In addition, it covers the two main categories of configuring the automation system hardware (non-networked and networked). Moreover, it compares a LAN-based to a WAN-based configuration and describes the advantages and disadvantages of each, as well as making a distinction between the traditional file server and the client/server architecture. The client/server architecture has three main types (two-tier, three-tier, and thin clients). These types are described along with the advantages and disadvantages of each type. The chapter ends with an activity for the reader to use to gain familiarity with the hardware configuration employed in a media center or small library.

Chapter 4 discusses system selection, focusing on the selection of an integrated microcomputer-based automated system. The chapter describes the selection process, provides guidelines for preparing a Request for Proposal (RFP), and presents a sample RFP. The sample RFP covers essential specifications for the entire system as well as for each library function, including utilities, circulation, OPAC, cataloging, authority control, acquisitions, and serials. Although the software specifications are extensive, it is not possible to create one list of specifications that will apply to every media center or library; the specifications must be tailored for each automation project. Managers of an automation project may want to develop additional specifications and delete some of the ones included in the example. In addition, any of the specifications considered essential in Chapter 4 may be considered only desirable in some media centers or libraries. Managers must adapt the specifications to suit the needs and requirements of each media center or library. The chapter concludes by listing a few pitfalls to avoid during the selection process.

Chapter 5 delineates the various stages and activities related to preparing the collection for automation. Collection preparation may be performed in parallel with many tasks involved in system implementation. Collection preparation includes weeding, inventory, and shelflist analysis. Database creation, which is accomplished through retrospective conversion (recon) of the shelflist, is described in detail. This discussion covers the various options for accomplishing recon, the method of achieving each option, and the advantages and disadvantages of each. It includes two new options for in-house conversion—import of MARC 21 records using fee-based Web services and Web-based free records—and delineates the advantages and disadvantages of each option. Of most importance is the cost analysis of vendor versus in-house recon options; this comparison shows the high cost of the latter. This chapter also provides essential specifications for the process, regardless of the conversion method used. These specifications can also be used for ordering MARC 21 records from book vendors.

Chapter 5 also covers bibliographic standards central to automation. MARC 21 components are described in detail and *Anglo-American Cataloguing Rules, Second Revised Edition (AACR2R)* and International Standard Bibliographic Description (ISBD) are included. Procedures for barcoding the collection are provided. The chapter ends with an activity for practicing cost analysis for recon.

Chapter 6 includes the processes important to implementing an automated system, including site preparation, which includes selection and placement of hardware, printers, and furniture; system installation; and testing. System maintenance, such as caring for computer equipment, system backup, and system security, has been given special attention. Staff and patron training is covered. Crucial to this chapter is a discussion of the process of database maintenance, which describes the most important MARC 21 fields that require attention, such as the Leader, fixed field, author field, title field, subject headings fields, and added entry fields. An activity about database maintenance appears at the end of this chapter.

Networking the media center or library—that is, connecting a set of computers to form a local area network (LAN) or joining a wide area network (WAN) for the purpose of sharing software—has become common. Networking may be performed in parallel with other tasks involved in system implementation. Chapter 7 presents types of networks, devices used to connect networks (e.g., repeaters, hubs, bridges, routers), and network components (cabling, topology, architecture, and protocols). It compares cabling options and describes various types of telephone connections (dedicated and dial-up) and elaborates on some of the digital leased telephone lines (ISDN, DSL, and T-1). The various designs or layouts of a network (bus, star, and ring) are described and illustrated in figures. In addition, the three most common LAN architectures (i.e., Ethernet, Token Ring, and Fiber Distributed Data Interface) are covered. A new section on network protocols, such as Transmission Control Protocol/Internet Protocol (TCP/IP), is included. The chapter lists selected companies that supply networking products. An activity about networking appears at the end of this chapter.

The new chapter on system migration (Chapter 8) describes the process of migration, including database cleanup, database analysis, database completion, and data migration. It recommends writing a Request for Proposal (RFP) when migrating from one system to another or when upgrading from an existing system to another. Chapter 8 also includes migration tips and advice for maintaining a smooth migration. The chapter concludes with an activity for the reader to use to gain experience in various activities involved in system migration.

The Web has transformed media centers and libraries into virtual hubs of information. There is no doubt that maintaining a presence on the Web has become the "norm." Hytelnet, which is a directory of telnet sites on the Internet, and which was the main vehicle for making OPACs available on the Internet, has become obsolete. Today, access to OPACs is via the Web. Chapter 9 describes how to make OPACs accessible via the Web, as well as how to access such OPACs. In addition, this chapter discusses the Z39.50 standard, which is central to searching various types of OPACs, regardless of software and hardware employed. The chapter delineates the benefits of making OPACs available on the Web. It ends with an activity for accessing the Z39.50 OPACs on the Web.

Chapter 10 discusses major recent developments in library automation. It elaborates on trends and issues that third-generation OPACs present. Also discussed is the role information professionals should play in providing and supporting effective user access. The chapter makes the point that these professionals should act as consultants, trainers, and information managers. Because they know their users and interact with them on a regular basis, information professionals should collaborate with system designers to enhance and build interfaces to OPACs that support user information seeking.

# ACTIVITIES

Eight activities are included in this book. Most have been field-tested by students in a class called Library Automation. Educators should modify the activities to suit the needs of their students.

# A NOTE ON TERMINOLOGY

The following terms have special meaning as used in this book. *Media specialist* is used for both school library media specialist and school librarian. *Information professional* is used to refer to practitioners in small libraries other than media centers. *Media center* is used for both the school library and school library media center. *Library* indicates a small library.

The URLs in this book were last accessed October 29, 2001, unless otherwise noted.

# Chapter 1

## Overview of Automated Systems

Prior to the 1970s, library automated systems were dedicated to a single function designed for a single-purpose operation. The circulation function was the first library operation to be automated due to its repetitive, routine, and time-consuming, multifaceted tasks (e.g., check-in, check-out, fines, overdue notices, and record keeping). In the late 1970s and early 1980s, vendors of automated systems introduced the Online Public Access Catalog (OPAC) function to existing circulation systems. By the late 1980s, integrated automation systems, those that combine circulation, OPACs, and cataloging, had become widely accepted in large libraries (Saffady 1999). These systems operated on mainframe and miniframe computers. The high cost of these computers and of the automation software were beyond the reach of many media centers and small libraries.

The proliferation of microcomputers in the early 1980s provided an incentive to automate media centers and small libraries. Computer Cat, an Apple II microcomputer-based online catalog, was the first automated system to be introduced in a media center. Developed by Colorado Computer Systems in 1981 for Mountain View Elementary School in Colorado, the system comprised three main components: OPAC, cataloging, and inventory (Costa 1981; Costa 1982). Computer Cat OPAC was a replica of the card catalog; it provided author, title, and subject searching capabilities.

In 1985, only 130 school sites had implemented stand-alone circulation and catalog systems (Murphy 1988). During the next few years, microcomputer processing and storage capacity increased while the price of hardware plummeted. This provided a unique opportunity for automation vendors to develop automation software to operate on microcomputers. Integrated microcomputer-based automated systems that support single and multi-user configurations and that combine multiple functions (i.e., OPAC, cataloging, circulation, acquisitions, and serials) were introduced before the end of the decade. A 1999 survey of more than 500 school libraries showed that 71 percent had an OPAC, 83 percent had an online circulation system, and 70 percent had both an OPAC and an online circulation system (Miller and Shontz 1999).

The introduction of online public access catalogs (OPACs) into libraries has had a marked impact on the way users access and retrieve information. This powerful information tool has allowed media specialists and information professionals to provide more effective and efficient information services.

The term *online catalog* refers to the entire software. *OPAC* is commonly used to refer to the public access module. The two terms are also used interchangeably. Today, OPACs are also referred to as Windows-based OPACs, Web-based OPACs, public access catalogs (PACs), Internet public access catalogs (IPACs), and Web public access catalogs (Web PACs). Regardless of the name used, a public access catalog is *not* a replica of the card catalog or a card catalog online. Rather, it is a tool with a seamless web of functions and services. See Chapter 10 for discussion of the latest developments in OPACs.

The microcomputer-based automation marketplace has grown rapidly, and microcomputer-based automated systems have been widely accepted in small- and medium-sized school, public, academic, and special libraries. The popularity of these systems is due to decline in the cost of hardware and software, the integration of a seamless "web" of information resources and services, the continuous augmentation of software search features and capabilities, the increased migration to Windows™ and World Wide Web interfaces, software compatibility with both PC and Macintosh platforms, and the use of powerful operating systems (e.g., Microsoft Windows NT™).

Currently, small- and medium-sized libraries have many automation software choices. *Library Journal* (Barry 2000), for example, lists the following automation companies, those that had the highest market share: Book Systems (Concourse), Companion (Alexandria), Sagebrush (Athena and Winnebago Spectrum), Follett (Circulation/Catalog Plus), and Sirs Mandarin (Mandarin M3 System). In a review of integrated automation software suitable for small school, academic, and public libraries, Beiser (1999a) described the following companies and the systems they offer: CASPR, Inc. (LibraryWorld), Chancery Software (Library Pro), Kelowna Software (Library 4 Universal), New Generation Technologies (LibrarySoft), and Surpass Software (Surpass). In another review, Beiser (1999b) included software packages suitable for small special, academic, and public libraries: Comstow Information Services, Inc. (BiblioTech Pro), Daikon Systems (PCCCWin), Electronic Online Systems (EOS) International (GLAS), Inmagic, Inc. (DB/TextWorks Library Guide, Keystone Systems, Inc. (KLAS), Lex Systems, Inc. (LexiFile, LexWin), The Library Corporation (Library.Solution), MC2 Systems (Auto Librarian), and One Point, Inc. (TLC).

# MODULES AND THEIR FUNCTIONS

The three basic modules in an automated system are public access, cataloging, and circulation. Public access, or the OPAC, is what users consult to find and retrieve information of interest. Generally, the OPAC is equivalent to the card catalog, but it provides advanced search features. The OPAC function allows searching by author, title, subject, or keyword; searches using Boolean operators (AND, OR, NOT); hyperlink searching (i.e., to find related records under specific words or subjects of interest that appear in a record); wild character searching (i.e., word truncation); and combined search strategy options (e.g., author-title; author-subject). The OPAC module is the only one that is inseparable from cataloging. A library cannot have the OPAC without the cataloging module, because the cataloging module is the database that houses all material records and makes them available in the OPAC. Therefore, the cataloging module is the heart of the automated system.

The cataloging function is accomplished in the cataloging module. This module performs various cataloging tasks, such as original cataloging using the Machine-Readable Cataloging (MARC) protocol, editing, copying, saving, and retrieving cataloged records. When a record is saved in the cataloging database, the record automatically appears in the OPAC, and a brief copy of the record is also generated automatically for the circulation module.

The circulation module performs the tasks involved in the circulation function, such as material check-in, check-out, inventory, overdue notices, holds and reserves, fines, and statistical reports.

An automated system may have additional modules, such as acquisitions, serials, and interlibrary loan. The acquisitions function is performed in the acquisitions module. It includes tasks such as material requests, purchase orders, material receipt, budget, vendor performance tracking, and record keeping. The serials function is achieved in the serials module. It covers tasks such as periodical subscription, acquisitions, routing, claiming, cancellation, budget, tracking vendor performance, and record keeping. The interlibrary loan function is accomplished in the interlibrary loan module. This module performs various tasks for borrowing and lending of materials among libraries.

The circulation, acquisitions, serials, and interlibrary loan modules function independently of one another in a stand-alone automated system, but they may operate both independently of and concurrently with one another in an integrated automated system. The module that is common to all functions, in both integrated and stand-alone systems, is the utilities module, which is mainly used to diagnose and address problems in the automated system's database. Tasks performed in this module include, but are not limited to, checking the database integrity; rebuilding database files, subject headings files, and file indexes; and backing up the database files.

# INTEGRATED OR STAND-ALONE?

Automated systems can be described by function, interface, and platform. In terms of function, systems can be stand-alone or integrated. In terms of interface, systems can be character-based, Windows-based, and Web-based. In terms of platform, systems can support PCs and/or Macintosh. An automated system that is either stand-alone or integrated can be Windows-based and/or Web-based and may operate on a PC and/or a Macintosh computer.

A stand-alone system includes one or more modules that represent library functions (e.g., circulation or cataloging and public access) that do not share a common bibliographic database. In other words, each stand-alone module works independently of other modules available in the automated system. An integrated system is a suite of interrelated modules that perform a variety of library functions (e.g., circulation, cataloging, public access, acquisitions, and serials) and share a common database. Each module in an integrated system works independently of and concurrently with other modules provided in the automated system. In 1997, the concept of "integration" took on a new meaning (Barry, Bilal, and Penniman 1998). Automation vendors have integrated new markets, new systems, and resources while maintaining current offerings (e.g., Java, Dublin Core, Graphical

User Interfaces [GUIs]) to respond to customer demands. In the K–12 marketplace, for example, Follett's "Schools Interoperability Framework" integrates various systems found in schools and school districts. Such integration aims at supporting school curricula, school libraries, administration, food service, and accounting.

An integrated automated system is preferred over a stand-alone system, even when only one module is purchased at a time. In an integrated system, as modules are added over time, they will share one common database and interface with one another. This interface provides users with improved services. With an integrated system that includes modules for the OPAC, cataloging, circulation, serials, and interlibrary loan, for example, a user who locates an item of interest in the OPAC can obtain the bibliographic information and the call number. The user can also determine the status of that item (e.g., check-out date, due date, on reserve), a service provided through the circulation module. In addition, the user can ascertain whether the item being searched in the OPAC is on order, received, claimed, canceled, or sent to the bindery, a service provided through the serials module. If a user does not find an item of interest in the OPAC, the user may issue a request for interlibrary loan to obtain the item from a library that has it, a service provided through the interlibrary loan module.

A media center or library with limited financial resources may acquire one module at a time. This decision must be based on the media center's or library's priorities for automation.

# BENEFITS OF LIBRARY AUTOMATION

The Web is making library automation the "norm" for all types of libraries. Any media center or library that is seeking to establish a presence on the Web must have its catalog automated. What is most evident about automation is that it improves library services and increases productivity, efficiency, and accuracy in performing a variety of library operations. Additional benefits of library automation are that:

- It allows patrons to use search strategies that exceed those that can be used with card catalogs. Card catalogs can be searched only by author, title, and subject; OPACs can be accessed by author, title, subject, and keyword. In addition, users can extend their search by using Boolean operators (AND, OR, NOT) and by combining search strategies (e.g., title and author, subject and author). In addition, OPAC users may limit their search results by such features as publication date, type of material (e.g., magazine, book, video), language, or reading level, and they can sort bibliographies by author, title, and publication date.

- The Windows-based OPACs allow for hyperlink searching, a new feature that was not possible in character-based systems (i.e., DOS). Through a hyperlink search a user can find related records in the automated system's database under a word or subject. The user can also locate related resources that appear on the Web via the MARC field 856 when this field is activated. Another search feature that was not possible in character-based systems is the visual search. An OPAC that has a Graphical User Interface (GUI) capability allows users to click on icons that represent functions instead of clicking on command buttons only. The visual representation of search functions is very attractive to young children especially, because visual interfaces that are based on pictures or icons are usually augmented with colors and easy-to-read text.

- It allows patrons to search the library's collection from locations outside the library's walls. Patrons who are equipped with a computer and a modem can dial into the OPAC from home, an office, or another remote location. Most automation software is compatible with the Z39.50 standard. Having this standard allows users to search OPACs on the Web using common interfaces and/or search features. This means that regardless of the automation software, operating system (e.g. Unix, Windows, Windows NT), or computer platform (PC or Macintosh) users have, they can search these OPACs using common search interfaces.

- It provides users with timely access to library materials. Library materials can be placed on shelves as soon as items are processed and MARC records are downloaded into a database. When MARC records are purchased with material orders, they eliminate the need for time-consuming original cataloging.

- It supports new means of information retrieval by introducing patrons to global information. The popularity and success of OPACs make them ideal to coexist with CD-ROM databases, online databases, the Web, and other information systems on a library's computer. A Z39.50-compliant OPAC allows users to search Z39.50-compliant databases using the search syntax of the OPAC, thereby eliminating the need to learn each database's search syntax.

- It eliminates routine tasks or performs them more efficiently. The circulation function, which includes check-in, check-out, overdue notices, and inventory, is tedious, repetitive, and time-consuming. Automating these functions can save a tremendous amount of time.

- It expedites and simplifies the inventory of library materials. The automated inventory is performed by scanning each item's barcode using a hand-held device, downloading scanned items into the automated system, and generating a variety of customized reports. In a non-automated environment, this procedure involves checking a shelflist card against the respective item on the shelf, flagging the shelflist cards for missing items, and generating inventory reports manually. The collection inventory that takes two months to complete in a non-automated environment may take two weeks in an automated environment.

- It encourages cooperative collection development and resource sharing (e.g., interlibrary loan). Automated media centers and libraries can develop a union catalog and join bibliographic utilities and consortia. A user who does not find an item of interest in the library's local OPAC may identify the libraries in the union catalog or consortia that have it. The user can then borrow the item through interlibrary loan or by checking it out from a designated library.

- It enables media centers and libraries to import and export MARC records. Records obtained from book vendors or other sources on disk are imported into an automated system to save cataloging time. Records can be exported from one system and imported into a new automated system without incurring new costs for retrospective conversion. Exporting records is essential for migrating from one automated system to another.

- It reduces (in integrated systems) the amount of time spent on material acquisition, serials management, budget administration, and record keeping.

- It motivates patrons, equips them with problem-solving and information retrieval skills, and provides them with lifelong learning experiences. In addition, it reinforces a positive attitude about the media center or library and improves the image of the media specialist or information professional. Patrons view the media center or library as an indispensable place for gaining access to global information and consider the media specialist or information professional a powerful information provider.

- It allows for cataloging Internet resources and for importing them into a local system. Automated systems also include tag 856 to link URLs to MARC 21 records. Although these features enhance a media center's or library's collection, they do present some problems. Internet resources are volatile and stateless, so they require validation on a regular basis. If such validation is performed in-house, it becomes very time consuming. Many automation vendors have provided solutions to this dilemma. One of these is to subscribe to an off-line URL service (monthly or quarterly) to obtain suitable URLs on CD-ROM or other media. The problem with this solution is that by the time the CD-ROM arrives, some of the URLs may have already vanished. Another solution is subscribing to an online URL service. A vendor hosts the URLs on a server and updates them constantly. Every URL that is activated in a media center's or library's local automated system passes through the vendor's server of URLs for validation before it is requested from the Internet/Web. This service is more up-to-date than the off-line service, but may be more costly.

- It can be used in collection mapping. Many automated systems have the capability to create collection maps to use for collection development. In consortia, creating such maps manually becomes very tedious and time consuming.

# DISADVANTAGES OF LIBRARY AUTOMATION

Even though you may have no doubt about automating your media center or library, it is important that you be aware of the disadvantages library automation may bear. These include the following:

- It is time-consuming. Planning, selecting, and implementing an automated system requires a significant, long-term commitment of staff time. Once selected and implemented, an automated system must be maintained on a regular basis. Having the automated system networked to a library's local area network (LAN) adds more demands on the media specialist's or information professional's time.

- It is costly. Start-up costs, software, hardware, network cabling, wiring, and software; furniture; ongoing expenses such as supplies for printers and barcode labels; annual maintenance and technical support; and conversion of a library's shelflist into a machine-readable format (i.e., MARC) may be more than many media centers and small libraries can afford.

- The demands of the automated system may not leave staff adequate time to provide new services or to work with students, teachers, and other clients. In fact, automation eliminates some tasks but generates new ones. End-user training, ongoing troubleshooting of hardware and software, and database maintenance place demands on the media specialist or information professional.

- Access to the automated system is unavailable during system downtime. This will hamper user access to the collection, especially if the card catalog or the shelflist no longer exists in the media center or library.

Awareness of the benefits and pitfalls of library automation will help you better prepare for the changes in your work duties. Library automation, like any technology, is costly in terms of time and money, and frustration and anguish are typical symptoms of technostress.

# REFERENCES

Barry, Jeff. 2000. Automated system marketplace 2000: Delivering the personalized library. *Library Journal* 125 (April 1): 49-60.

Barry, Jeff, Dania Bilal, and W. David Penniman. 1998. Automated system marketplace: The competitive struggle. *Library Journal* 123 (April 1): 43-52.

Beiser, Karl. 1999a. Integrated library system software for smaller libraries, part 1. Special, academic, and public libraries. *Library Technology Reports* 35 (2): 119-262.

————. 1999b. Integrated library system software for smaller libraries, part 2. School, academic, and public libraries. *Library Technology Reports* 35 (4): 365-548.

Costa, Betty. 1981. Microcomputers in Colorado—It's elementary. *Wilson Library Bulletin* 55 (May): 676-717.

————. 1982. An online catalog for an elementary school library media center. *School Library Media Quarterly* 10 (Summer): 337-46.

Miller, Marilyn Lea, and Marilyn L. Shontz. 1999. How do you measure up? *School Library Journal* 45 (October): 50-60.

Murphy, Catherine. 1988. The time is right to automate. *School Library Journal* 35 (November): 42-47.

Saffady, William. 1999. *Introduction to automation for librarians*. 4th ed. Chicago: American Library Association.

# Chapter 2

## Preparing for Automation

Automation involves a spectrum of activities that is much broader than selection and implementation of a system. To prepare for the automation project, media specialists and information professionals should identify the mission and goals of the host organization as they relate to the media center or library, acquire adequate knowledge of the automation process, develop an understanding of various library functions, access staff needs and user information needs, and examine the sources of funding for the automation project.

Staff who are engaged in an automation project must possess adequate knowledge about a wide range of topics, including:

> evaluating, selecting, and implementing an automated system;
>
> software and hardware terminology;
>
> automated systems' functional specifications;
>
> user information-seeking behavior and information needs; and
>
> the various operations of the media center or library.

Important features of automation to learn include the following:

- The benefits and pitfalls of library automation. Chapter 1 discusses this topic.

- The impact of automation on the organizational structure in general and on the media center or library in particular. Such impacts may include access to the OPAC from offices, homes, and other remote locations; the kind of services that may be eliminated, refined, or created; changes in staff responsibilities; and the need to create new positions and eliminate or redefine existing ones.

- Issues and problems related to using OPACs. Research has shown that both children and adults experience difficulties in using OPACs (Borgman 1996; Borgman et. al. 1995; Wildemuth and O'Neill 1995; Solomon 1993; Kuhlthau 1993; Jacobson 1991; Chen 1991; Blazek and Bilal 1988). Being aware of the common problems users experience in using OPACs provides guidance for selecting an automated system that meets users' information needs and supports their information seeking. It will also offer a framework for media specialists and information professionals for designing effective user training after implementing an OPAC.

- The various automation software suitable for the media center or library to be automated, including the modules available, the modules that have recently been added, and the strengths and weaknesses of each module.

- General historical background and financial information about the companies that support the most popular systems. The financial stability of the companies is especially important.

- The automated systems vendors' present and future efforts in implementing new technologies (e.g., Java, Dublin Core), latest standards (e.g., MARC 21, Z39.50), Web and Windows interfaces, and cross-platform applications (PC and Macintosh).

# KNOWLEDGE ACQUISITION

Learning about automation is vital for the success of the automation project. One can learn more about automation by researching the library literature. "The Automated System Marketplace," an annual survey of companies that supply automation software and services, appears in the April 1 issue of *Library Journal*. This survey has a profile of select automation companies, the software they offer, the automation and related services they provide, the recent products they have released, the latest technologies they have implemented, and the products and/or services they will be developing. For example, the April 1, 2000, issue briefly describes (but does not evaluate) twenty-six software packages suitable for all types of libraries (Barry 2000). For a thorough evaluation of various software packages, consult *Library Technology Reports*. The July-August 1999 issue of this journal contains a comprehensive evaluation of ten automation software packages suitable for small school, public, and academic libraries (Beiser 1999).

For additional, detailed descriptions of various types of software, consult the *Directory of Library Automation Software, Systems, and Services,* compiled and edited by Pamela Cibbarelli (2000). This biannual directory describes and compares microcomputer, minicomputer, and mainframe software packages. It also provides detailed analysis of each package, such as software and hardware requirements, compatibility with bibliographic standards, components, applications, search features, and price.

## Learning from Colleagues

Communicating with colleagues in person or via listservs, such as **LM_NET** (http://ericir.syr.edu/lm_net/sub.html), to ask for advice or to share successful and unsuccessful automation experiences will provide insight into the strengths and weaknesses of selected automated systems. Subscribing to technology-oriented mailing lists or newspapers is another good way to learn from the experienced and the expert. If possible, it is a good idea to form a partnership with a nearby library that has recently undergone automation; this will allow you to learn about that library's successes and failures.

Other listservs to consult are the Association of Educational Communications and Technology (AECT) (http://www.aect.org), Library and Information Science Forum (http://web.utk.edu/~gwhitney/jesse.html), and Special Library Association Discussion List (http://www.sla.org/ content/Help/discussion/index.cfm).

## Learning at Conferences and from Vendors

People new to automation should attend workshops or sessions at conferences to learn the basics. Attending vendors' product review sessions at state and national conferences allows you to preview software packages. Early in the preparation process, such previews will help you to understand the various features that automation has to offer. Later in the process, after some software packages have been selected for consideration, you will preview these software packages on site. At that point, inviting companies to provide demonstrations of their automated systems will clarify the systems' functions and capabilities and thus help you to evaluate automated systems. Learning about software features is not enough, however; you will also want to research each company's financial stability, service, products, reliability, and experience. Automation companies may go out of business, shift their priorities from automation, or sell their software to other companies.

# NEEDS ASSESSMENT

Needs assessment is the second step in preparing for automation. It is conducted to analyze and evaluate the current media center's or library's services, procedures, and functions to improve productivity, effectiveness, and efficiency. It is also conducted to assess staff and user needs. Needs assessment will also help determine how people will be affected by the technological change.

## Staff Needs

All forms of change may be accompanied by a number of fears, of which the most common are fear of the unknown, of economic insecurity, of changed relationships in the workplace, of changed working practices, of computers, and of increased management surveillance (Morris and Dyer 1998). Managers of the automation project should strengthen their leadership skills, develop an understanding of change, and assume the role of change agents whose task it is to provide support and create an environment that lowers the barriers to change. An assessment of staff needs will reveal their concerns, their current roles and responsibilities, their level of job satisfaction, and their openness to change. It will provide a framework for defining existing problems, diagnosing future problems, re-evaluating job descriptions, and reassigning responsibilities.

The success of the automation project depends not only on the proper operation of the software and hardware used but also on staff and user responses. Therefore, staff involvement is crucial to the success of an automated project. Well-trained staff can assist with many tasks, such as needs assessment, data collection, shelflist preparation, and collection inventory. Staff should be provided with the opportunity to acquire the necessary knowledge of the automation process.

Because automation affects all staff members, it is important that they be involved in the decision-making process. This involvement will reduce job insecurity, foster confidence in performing new activities, and garner staff support. It is recommended that staff be included on the automation advisory committee. (The need for an automation advisory committee is discussed below.)

## User Needs

Users include students or clients, administrators, teachers, and other staff. Users' responses to the technological change will vary. "Some will be enthusiastic to see new features and will even push the library to move ahead. Others will be resistant to losing what they have come to know and trust" (Morris and Dyer 1998, 305). A needs assessment survey of users will indicate their information needs, their concerns about automation, and possible problem areas that must be addressed. Like staff, users need to be educated about automation. The media specialist or information professional should consider providing a workshop about automation to users. In addition, involving users in the automation project may alleviate their fear and, subsequently, will create a positive environment in the workplace.

## Role of the Automation Advisory Committee

It is recommended that an automation advisory committee be formed. The committee is responsible for planning and coordinating the automation project from start to finish. This includes data gathering, needs assessment, researching the literature, attending conferences and seminars, preparing the media center or library for automation, developing a Request for Proposal (RFP), evaluating RFPs, and selecting and implementing the automated system.

The committee should include representatives from staff and users, as well as media specialists and information professionals. It should also include the technology coordinator or other personnel in the workplace who have expertise in information technology. Be careful when working with computer experts; although their expertise is essential, "it does not confer insight into the best way to automate library functions and deliver library services" (Beiser 1999, 370). This means that media specialists and information professionals should be the ones to make the final decision about the automated software to adopt.

## Questions to Ask in the Needs Assessment

Understanding the mission and goals of the media center or library in relation to those of the host organization is an integral component of needs assessment. Some questions to address during the assessment process follow:

- What are the host organization's present and future technology priorities?

- What are the media center's or library's present and future technology priorities?

- What media center or library services and procedures can be improved through automation?

• How will automation increase media center or library staff productivity, accuracy, and efficiency?

• Are there alternatives to automation that may equally improve services, procedures, and productivity?

Automation is time-consuming and costly. Engaging in an automation project requires a long-term commitment of staff and financial resources. Clarifying the goals and objectives of the media center or library at the outset is essential to avoid unnecessary expenditures. As Wright (1995) notes: "No library can afford to indulge in activities which cost money and take staff time unless these activities are directly related to library goals and objectives" (9).

The needs assessment process includes function analysis, data gathering, and data analysis and interpretation.

## Function Analysis

The first step in a needs assessment is to analyze each existing media center or library function. Typical functions include circulation, cataloging, and information service. Each function and task should be analyzed and evaluated in relation to the procedures used to accomplish it.

The circulation function includes material check-out and check-in, overdues, fines, inventory, reserve, renewal, and report management. The cataloging function involves cataloging a variety of items in-house or ordering preprocessed catalog cards when items are purchased. When in-house cataloging is performed in a non-automated setting, catalog cards may be produced on the premises or be purchased. The information service function provides service to patrons to meet their information needs. These needs can be met by using the card catalog or other bibliographic tools available in the media center or library.

To develop a clear understanding of the procedures involved in each function, it is useful to draw and compare two diagrams of the most important workflow patterns, with one workflow diagram showing how the procedure is accomplished in a non-automated environment and the other showing how it is accomplished in an automated environment

Figure 2.1 shows that filing check-out cards is time consuming and may incur errors. Automating this function (see Figure 2.2) would save staff time filing because the cards are eliminated and barcodes are scanned to check-out materials. A high accuracy rate is achieved because the automation system files checked-out items.

Figure 2.3 shows that the task in which problems may occur in a non-automated check-in function is finding the card for a checked-out item. Such an item is usually filed and kept in a material check-out box. Retrieving a card from this box may be time-consuming, especially if it is misfiled. One may have to go through the entire box to find the misfiled card. In an automated environment, however, this task is simplified and is less time-consuming, because when an employee scans the returned item's barcode the system purges it from the checked-out materials module (see Figure 2.4).

Another time-consuming task is collection inventory. Figure 2.5 displays the various tasks involved in performing this function. Each task performed (2, 3, and 4) will take time and most likely incur errors. Again, using an automated system to perform the inventory will be more time effective and will result in a much higher accuracy rate (see Figure 2.6). The report the automated system prepares when a full or partial inventory of a collection is completed is definitely much more accurate than the report that a media specialist or information professional could prepare manually or by using spreadsheets.

Remember that automation has many benefits and that it is not carried out only to save time filing or producing cards.

**Figure 2.1. Circulation function: Non-automated item check-out task.**

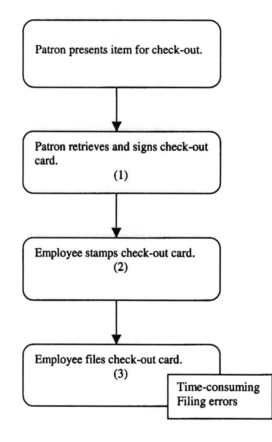

**Figure 2.2. Circulation function: Automated item check-out task.**

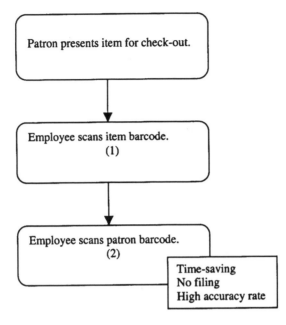

**Figure 2.3. Circulation function: Non-automated item check-in task.**

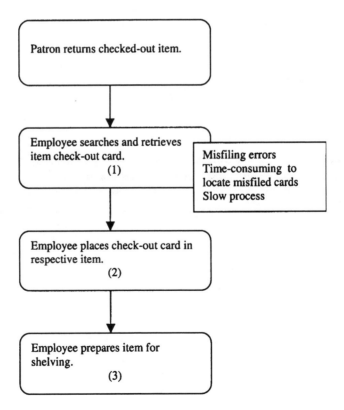

### Figure 2.4. Circulation function: Automated item check-in task.

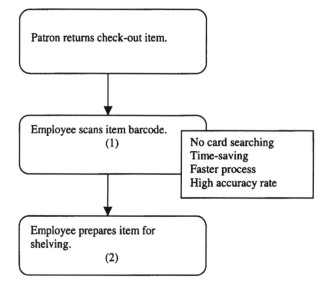

### Figure 2.5. Inventory function: Non-automated inventory task.

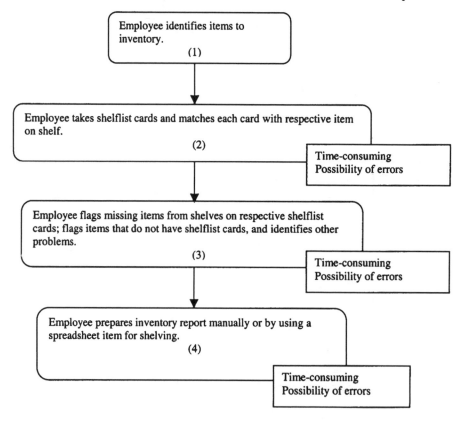

## Figure 2.6. Inventory function: Automated inventory task.

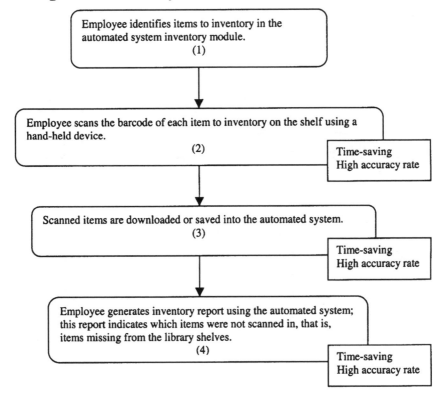

## Data Gathering

The second step in needs assessment is gathering quantitative data about each function; this information is used first to justify the automation of each function and second to set priorities for automating the various functions. Tables 2.1 through 2.5 illustrate guidelines for data collection. To use these forms in gathering data, decide whether to collect data on a weekly, monthly, or annual basis and use a checkmark to indicate the appropriate category. As applicable, provide the number of operations for each task; the frequency, or how many times the task is done in the time period you selected (weekly, monthly, or annually); and the accuracy, preferably expressed as a percentage, of accomplishing the task. If a criterion does not apply to a task, write *N/A* (not applicable) in the appropriate cell. Calculate the total or average number of activities or tasks, the time it takes to achieve them, frequency in performing them, and accuracy in completing them.

## Table 2.1.
## Data Gathering Scheme for the Circulation Function

Weekly_____          Monthly_____          Annually_____

| Tasks | Number | Time | Frequency | Accuracy |
|---|---|---|---|---|
| Item check-out | | | | |
| Item check-out card filed | | | | |
| Misfiling of item check-out | | | | |
| Item check-in | | | | |
| Item check-in card filed | | | | |
| Backlogs in card filing | | | | |
| Overdues and fines composed | | | | |
| Reports generated for overdues and fines | | | | |
| Item inventory preparation | | | | |
| Inventory of items | | | | |
| Inventory problem areas (flagging missing items, etc.) | | | | |
| Inventory report generation | | | | |
| Item reservation/hold processed | | | | |
| Item reservation/hold notices sent | | | | |
| Equipment booking processed | | | | |
| Equipment booking notices sent | | | | |
| Other tasks: | | | | |
| Total/Average | | | | |

# Table 2.2.
# Data Gathering Scheme for the Cataloging Function

Weekly_____          Monthly_____          Annually_____

| Tasks | Number | Time | Frequency | Accuracy |
|---|---|---|---|---|
| Print items cataloged in-house | | | | |
| Nonprint items cataloged in-house | | | | |
| Catalog cards produced in-house | | | | |
| Preprocessed catalog cards ordered | | | | |
| Backlogs in cataloging | | | | |
| Card filing in the card catalog | | | | |
| Reports generated for in-house cataloging | | | | |
| Other tasks: | | | | |
| Total/Average | | | | |

## Table 2.3.
## Data Gathering Scheme for the Information Service Function

Weekly_____          Monthly_____          Annually_____

| Tasks | Number | Time | Frequency | Accuracy |
|---|---|---|---|---|
| Patrons with library cards | | | | |
| Patrons who use the media center/library | | | | |
| Patrons who use the card catalog | | | | |
| Patrons who request reference assistance | | | | |
| Bibliography compilation or other activity using the card catalog (by staff) | | | | |
| Patron's use of the subject card catalog | | | | |
| Patron's success in using the subject card catalog | | | | |
| Patrons' use of the title card catalog | | | | |
| Patron's success in using the title card catalog | | | | |
| Patron's use of the author card catalog | | | | |
| Patron's success in using the author card catalog | | | | |
| Staff use of the card catalog (subject, author, and title) | | | | |
| Staff success in using the card catalog (subject, author, and title) | | | | |
| Other Tasks: | | | | |
| Total/Average | | | | |

# Table 2.4.
# Data Gathering Scheme for the Acquisitions Function

Weekly_____          Monthly_____          Annually_____

| Tasks | Number | Time | Frequency | Accuracy |
|---|---|---|---|---|
| Items requisition preparation | | | | |
| Items ordered | | | | |
| Fund encumbrance | | | | |
| Budget management | | | | |
| Items received | | | | |
| Items returned | | | | |
| Items claimed | | | | |
| Items canceled | | | | |
| Acquisitions reports generated | | | | |
| Record keeping (filing requests, tracking vendor performance, etc.) | | | | |
| Other Tasks: | | | | |
| Total/Average | | | | |

# Table 2.5.
# Data Gathering Scheme for the Serials Function

Weekly_____          Monthly_____          Annually_____

| Tasks | Number | Time | Frequency | Accuracy |
|---|---|---|---|---|
| Serials subscription | | | | |
| Serials checked-in | | | | |
| Serials routed | | | | |
| Serials claimed | | | | |
| Serials canceled | | | | |
| Serials renewed | | | | |
| Fund encumbrance | | | | |
| Budget management | | | | |
| Serials reports generated | | | | |
| Record keeping (filing requests, tracking vendor performance, etc.) | | | | |
| Other Tasks: | | | | |
| Total/Average | | | | |

## Data Analysis and Interpretation

The final activity in the needs assessment is analyzing the collected data in relation to the workflow patterns. This analysis will allow you to determine which functions to automate and in what order to automate them. Prioritizing the functions to be automated permits one to effectively allocate financial resources. This is especially important when a media center or library is experiencing budget constraints, because it allows the organization to reap the greatest results from its investment in automation. Typical questions to ask in determining priorities follow:

- Which tasks are the least productive?

- Which tasks are the most repetitive, labor-intensive, and time-consuming?

- Which tasks result in inaccuracy, inefficiency, and ineffectiveness?

If you find that the circulation function is the most tedious, demanding, and repetitive, for example, and that there is a need to increase its effectiveness, accuracy, and efficiency, then that function is a prime candidate for automation. Similarly, if a user survey indicates that the greatest demand or need is to assist users in finding information and to improve access to the collection, then public access is the highest priority. It is worth noting that the public access function, which is supported by the OPAC in an automated environment, cannot be implemented without the cataloging function; this gives OPAC and cataloging functions equal priority.

Data collection and analysis are useful, even when funds are available to automate all functions and, therefore, prioritization is not needed. In this case, the data provide a framework for establishing essential specifications that meet the media center's or library's needs and requirements. The data may indicate, for example, that patrons using the card catalog have difficulty retrieving information by subject. In this case, the subject and keyword search capabilities of the automated systems under consideration must be evaluated as they relate to the user's needs.

# FUNDING

Automating for the purpose of saving money doesn't work. Automation improves library services; enhances access to the collection; and increases productivity, accuracy, and efficiency in performing tasks. Because automation saves time in executing tasks and rendering service, it may allow staff more time to help users and to create new services. Therefore, during the initial stages of the planning process, the focus should be on how to proceed with automation and what must accomplished rather than how much it costs (Wright 1995). After the benefits of automation are revealed and a justification for automation is established, the availability of monies or sources of funding can be investigated.

In seeking monies to fund an automation project, you may not seek funding for automating all functions at once. As mentioned previously, prioritizing functions provides guidance for phasing in automation, thus allowing for budget constraints.

## Sources of Funding

Automation may be state funded, supported by funds raised internally, or provided by external sources, such as local businesses, Friends of the Library groups, Parent Teacher Organization (PTOs), and private organizations and foundations.

Funding for the automation project should be assessed during the preparation process to determine what funds will be available for present and future support. If funds are not available to acquire all modules in an automated system, for example, consider phasing in the project by acquiring one module at a time, based on your priorities for automation. If funds are available, a decision may have to be made whether to hire an automation consultant to assist with the project. If you feel comfortable about gathering information and learning about the automation process, you may not need a consultant. Even when a consultant is hired, the final decision about selecting an automated system should lie with the automation advisory committee, not the consultant.

## Cost Estimates

Budgeting for the automation project requires a cost estimate for the overall project, including ongoing expenses. The cost estimate should include software, hardware, utilities, supplies, personnel, and ongoing expenses.

The cost estimate for software includes the automation software and other software that supports the operation of the automated system, such as software for barcode or label production, software for in-house retrospective conversion, or a Web browser to provide access to the OPAC on the Web.

Hardware may include computer stations, a host system or file server, printers, scanners, inventory devices, an uninterruptible power supply (UPS) for the file server, modems, and the hardware needed to create a local area network (LAN). The cost of the LAN will depend on the network topology (i.e., the cabling system) and network architecture (e.g., token ring, Ethernet) selected. For a more detailed discussion of LANs and the hardware required for them, see Chapter 7.

Utilities include retrospective conversion, Internet access, site licenses for multi-user access, update of existing wiring, installation of additional telephone lines, remodeling the facilities, and furniture.

Supplies are barcode labels for both materials and patrons, barcode protectors, library cards, due date cards, overdue notices, paper for printers, and the like. Supplies are also considered ongoing expenses.

Personnel costs include hiring a consultant, new staff, and certified personnel for cable installation or other tasks as needed. Personnel costs also cover staff training for attending automation workshops and training in the use of automation software after the system is implemented.

Ongoing expenses comprise software updates, technical support, software and hardware maintenance, telecommunications charges, and supplies. The costs of these project components can be found in product catalogs and by communicating with automation vendors.

# SUMMARY

Preparing for automation is an essential activity in the automation process. It involves knowledge acquisition, needs assessment, and budgeting. Knowledge acquisition is necessary to obtain adequate background about the automation process. Needs assessment is conducted to examine and evaluate the media center's or library's goals and objectives, procedures, and functions and to collect data about each function for the purpose of justifying and prioritizing its automation. Workflow diagrams provide a clear understanding of the task involved in each function. Needs assessment is also performed to determine user and staff needs. Automation does not save money. It is cost-effective, it increases productivity and efficiency, and it enhances access to the media center's or library's collection. The focus during planning should be on these benefits and on how to proceed with automation rather than on how much it costs.

# REFERENCES

Barry, Jeff. 2000. Automated system marketplace 2000: Delivering the personalized library. *Library Journal* 125 (April 1): 49-60.

Beiser, Karl. 1999. Integrated library system software for smaller libraries. Part 2. School, academic, and public libraries. *Library Technology Reports* 35 (4): 365-95.

Blazek, Ron, and Dania Bilal. 1988. Problems with OPAC: A case study of an academic research library. *RQ* 28 (2): 169-78.

Borgman, Christine. 1996. Why are online catalogs still hard to use? *Journal of the American Society for Information Science* 47 (7): 493-503.

Borgman, Christine, et al. 1995. Children's searching behavior on browsing and keyword online library catalog: The Science Library Catalog Project. *Journal of the American Society for Information Science* 46 (9): 663-84.

Chen, Shu-Hsien. 1991. A study of online catalog searching behavior of high school students. Ed.D. diss., University of Georgia.

Cibbarelli, Pamela, ed. 2000. *Directory of library automation software, systems, and Services (2000–2001)*. Medford, NJ: Information Today.

Jacobson, Francis F. 1991. Information retrieval systems and youth: A review of recent literature. *Journal of Youth Services in Libraries* 5 (Fall): 109-13.

Kuhlthau, Carol C. 1993. *Seeking meaning: A process approach to library and information services*. Norwood, NJ: Ablex.

Morris, Anne, and Hilary Dyer. 1998. *Human aspects of library automation*. 2d ed. Brookfield, VT: Gower.

Solomon, Paul, 1993. Children's information retrieval behavior: A case analysis of an OPAC. *Journal of the American Society for Information Science* 44 (5): 245-64.

Wildemuth, Barbara M., and Ann L. O'Neill. 1995. The "known" in known item searches: Empirical support for user-centered design. *College and Research Libraries* 56 (May): 265-81.

Wright, Keith C. 1995. *Computer-related technologies on library operations*. Brookfield, VT: Gower.

## *Activity: Data Gathering Analysis*

**Objective 1:** To analyze various workflow patterns and diagram them.
**Description:**

1.  Collect information about the procedures and workflow patterns of various functions and tasks performed in a non-automated media center or a small library. You may interview a media specialist or information professional to determine the patterns.

2.  Prepare a workflow diagram for each task performed for each function. Create a separate workflow diagram for each task in a function, with identifiable starting and stopping points. Represent the procedures for each task from start to finish. Enumerate each procedure on the diagram.

3.  Briefly describe each procedure illustrated in the diagram on a separate sheet.

**Objective 2:** To gather data about the functions of a media center or a small library; this information could be used to build arguments for automation and to prioritize the functions to be automated.
**Description:**

1.  Select a non-automated media center or a small library and describe

    Its mission and goals,

    The number of clients it serves,

    Existing user services,

    Collection size, and

    New services to be implemented.

2.  Gather data about the functions of the media center or small library using the forms in Tables 2.1 through 2.5 (pages 18–22).

3.  Examine the workflow diagrams developed for the first part of this activity. Link the collected data to the respective tasks.

4.  Determine the tasks that are most repetitive, tedious, and labor-intensive.

5.  Determine the tasks that may involve inaccuracy, inefficiency, and low productivity.

6.  Select functions for automation and justify your decision. Prioritize the functions and, again, justify your decision. If all functions are of equal priority, provide strong justification for your decision.

# Chapter 3

---

## System Architecture and
## Hardware Configurations

---

Automated systems software must be capable of performing simple and sophisticated tasks and must comply with the latest bibliographic standards. In this aspect, not all systems are created equal. Capabilities vary according to platform (Macintosh or IBM-PC compatible), operating system (e.g., Macintosh, Windows NT, Unix), the kind of computer (i.e., microcomputer, minicomputer, and mainframe) used, and system architecture. Capabilities refer to the functions or tasks an automated system can perform, the size of the collection it can accommodate, the number and size of patron records it can store, and its interface with other systems or tools (e.g., bibliographic utilities, the Web). Operating systems are software programs that monitor, supervise, and execute functions in a computer. In a network environment (e.g., local area network), Unix and Windows NT have become the most popular operating systems. An automated system may operate on a microcomputer, minicomputer, or mainframe computer. Generally, the differences among these computers are in the processing power, disk storage, memory size, number of terminals or computers supported, intended applications, and cost (Saffady 1999). Automation using miniframes and mainframes is beyond the scope of this book; however, many of the topics discussed here in relation to microcomputers will apply equally well, or with some adaptation, to media centers and small libraries that are networked to mainframes or miniframes.

The architectures that have characterized library automated systems are hierarchical and client/server. In a hierarchical architecture, all processing and tasks are controlled by the host system (a mainframe or miniframe computer). Remote computers that are connected to the host system emulate "dumb" terminals in communicating with the host system. These terminals have little or no processing capabilities, so they perform limited tasks such as input and output. In the late 1980s and early 1990s, a new computing model has emerged: the client/server. This model evolved from the proliferation of PC-based networks. The client/server model was initially designed to "downsize" existing hierarchical computing models that relied primarily on mainframe computers that are very expensive

**27**

(Haley 1998). The client/server model is geared toward less expensive hardware while using powerful operating systems such as Unix and Windows NT. Recently, most automation vendors, including those that develop software for the small library marketplace, have utilized a client/server architecture for the design of their automated systems. This architecture is based on the "open system" concept, which features standardized connectivity of software and hardware that different automated systems vendors offer (Boss 1997).

To select the best system for a specific automation project, one must match the needs, requirements, and financial resources of the media center or library to the capabilities and costs of the various hardware and software.

# MICROCOMPUTERS

Microcomputers are also known as personal, desktop, or portable computers. They are used in offices, homes, schools, laboratories, and other facilities. They can be used to support stand-alone, or independent, operations and to create a local area network (LAN) or a wide area network (WAN). A LAN is a set of interconnected hardware devices designed to share software and hardware peripherals. It is usually confined to a fairly small geographical area: one building, or a group of buildings close to each other. A WAN is a statewide, regional, nationwide, or worldwide network designed to share software, such as the Internet.

Most media centers and small libraries will use a microcomputer-based automation system. This book assumes a basic knowledge of microcomputers, but readers who require more information about them should refer to Ron White's *How Computers Work* (2002).

# AUTOMATION SOFTWARE FOR VARIOUS CLASSES OF COMPUTERS

Automation software may operate on mainframes, miniframes, or microcomputers. Some software is written especially for a certain type of computer (e.g., a mainframe); other software is compatible with more than one type of computer (i.e., it may run on both mainframes and microcomputers). Generally speaking, the automation software for miniframes and mainframes is designed to handle the high volume of operations generated in large academic, special, and public libraries or to support a shared automation system in a WAN environment. Most automated systems designed for use in media centers and small libraries are microcomputer-based. Recently, many medium-sized libraries have started to shift to microcomputer-based systems.

# OPTIONS FOR HARDWARE CONFIGURATIONS USING MICROCOMPUTERS

Hardware configurations for automated systems can be divided into two main categories: non-networked and networked. A non-networked configuration operates in a stand-alone environment, whereas a networked configuration requires that a LAN or WAN exist.

# Non-Networked Hardware Configuration

An automated system that operates in a non-networked environment may have a stand-alone configuration with either integrated or non-integrated automation software. A media center or library may have an automation software package installed on five computers, for example, but none of these computers shares a common automation database or the peripherals supported (e.g., printers). In other words, this configuration consists of one or more microcomputer stand-alone stations that function independently. The automation software is installed and updated on each computer's hard disk so that each computer holds everything it needs to perform automated functions. This configuration is found most often in a media center or library with a small collection, small number of users, or limited financial resources. Libraries that start automation with one module (e.g., circulation) may choose this hardware configuration. It is important to note that a stand-alone hardware configuration is different from a stand-alone software configuration. A stand-alone software configuration means that the software is non-integrated. For further discussion of integrated and non-integrated (stand-alone) software configuration, see Chapter 1.

There are distinct advantages to the stand-alone configuration. One is financial. Libraries that cannot afford a LAN may choose a stand-alone configuration. Other advantages pertain to operation and services. Because each computer operates independently, the malfunction of one computer will not affect the operation of others. In addition, because the database resides on the hard drive of the computer(s) in the library, the database can be updated as a new software version arrives.

However, the stand-alone configuration has a few disadvantages. The automation software must be installed and updated on each computer station rather than accessed from a server; this may add to the cost of the software. Updating the software must be done on each computer station. The more stations, the more time-consuming it is to install and update the software. In addition, problem diagnosis and software and hardware troubleshooting is time-consuming, especially when more than one or two computer stations malfunction at the same time, because each station may have different problems.

Another configuration that existed in a non-networked environment several years ago is the CD-ROM. This configuration is similar to the microcomputer stand-alone configuration, except that the automation software operated from one or more CD-ROMs rather than each computer's hard disk. To make this work, each computer station was equipped with a CD-ROM drive. This configuration was associated with the software rather than the hardware, meaning that the software was available on CD-ROM. Software vendors that used to develop OPACs on CD-ROMs no longer support this configuration (e.g., Brodart Automation at http://www.Brodart.com). The CD-ROM products that are still popular, however, are those that are geared for retrospective conversion (recon). Products such as Brodart's *Precision One*, the Library Corporation's *Bibliofile*, and Follett's *Alliance Plus* contain millions of MARC records that media specialists and information professionals can use to find record matches for converting their shelflists.

# Networked Hardware Configuration

A networked configuration for an automated system can be LAN-based or WAN-based. Both of these configurations may have software with a client/server architecture. A new trend for configuring an automated system is the access service provider (ASP).

In the ASP model, the database is stored on the automation vendor's server. The vendor acts as the ASP. Database update, problem diagnosis, and troubleshooting are performed by the vendor remotely. At the time of writing, this model has just emerged in the automation marketplace. The success of this model and its acceptance by librarians are yet to be determined.

# LAN-Based versus WAN-Based Configuration

In a LAN-based configuration the automation software is stored on a media center's or library's LAN server. In this case, the media center or library does not share its automated software with other libraries (e.g., in a school district), and all processing tasks (e.g., cataloging, import of MARC records, circulation records) are performed locally. In a WAN-based configuration, a media center's or library's automated software is stored on a WAN server in a centralized location and each media center or library in the WAN accesses the automation software remotely. In a WAN environment, all or most processing tasks are performed in a centralized location. A union catalog is an example of a shared automated system that operates over a WAN. Each of these configuration options has advantages and disadvantages. Media specialists or information professionals should evaluate the strengths and weaknesses of each option.

## *Advantages of LAN-Based and WAN-Based Configurations*

A LAN-based configuration has many advantages. The greatest of these is that the media center or library will have total control over its database, as well as software installation and updates. There are other benefits as well:

- Users may have faster access to the collection because cataloging and/or MARC record downloading is (are) performed locally.

- Problem diagnosis and hardware troubleshooting may be faster, especially if the media specialist or information professional is also a technology specialist.

- A media center's or library's OPAC can be available over the Web. Updates to the OPAC may be faster because they are performed locally. However, a Web-based OPAC may require setting up and maintaining a Web server.

- Users see only the local media center or library's holdings, whereas they will be able to see the holdings of multiple libraries in a WAN system. The latter may cause problems if users are not well trained in how to identify local holdings.

The major advantages of a WAN-based configuration follow:

- A WAN-based automation system will allow users to have access to holdings of multiple media centers or libraries. Provided that users are well trained in using the OPAC in a WAN environment, they will be able to search local and/or all holdings in the union catalog that runs over the WAN. When an interlibrary loan feature is available online, a user will be able to issue an automated interlibrary loan form for requesting a specific item. The availability of a union catalog provides a richer collection for users.

- The cataloging of library materials in-house may result in higher quality MARC records and consistency in cataloging, especially if the staff members who catalog these materials at the central location are well trained in performing this task. When the central location in a WAN-based system has access to a bibliographic utility, such as the Online Computer Library Center (OCLC), copy cataloging can be performed, thereby reducing the time it takes to do original cataloging.

- Software may be more economical in a WAN than in a LAN environment.

### Disadvantages of LAN-Based and WAN-Based Configurations

The LAN-based configuration has certain disadvantages. The primary ones follow:

- A limited collection is available to users because they can only see the local holdings.

- Although control over the local database is an advantage, it can also be a disadvantage. Media specialists and information professionals will have to assume the responsibility of database backups, database and server maintenance, software installation and updates, and hardware troubleshooting. These tasks require adequate knowledge and skills to perform effectively and efficiently.

There are disadvantages to WAN-based configurations, also:

- Fast access to information may be compromised due to high traffic over the WAN. A reliable telecommunications connection is a necessity in a shared system over a WAN.

- Because all client computers are connected to servers at the central location, they will all be affected when the servers are down. In this case, user assistance is hampered and a media specialist or information professional will not be able to seek the help needed to fulfill users' needs from neighborhood libraries that share the same automation system in the WAN.

- Learning how to use a shared automated system in a WAN environment may be more complex than learning one's local system. This is because the shared system may have added features that are not available in a local system.

## CLIENT/SERVER ARCHITECTURE

Regardless of the configuration option a media center or library may have, the software architecture to consider for a networked configuration is the client/server. A client/server architecture is a computing environment that divides the functions or application processing between a client's computer (desktop) and the application server (provider) to which the client's computer is connected (Boss 1998). The server is a dedicated, high-end microcomputer station that is used to optimize requests that are issued by the clients. Multiple servers may exist on a LAN (e.g., application servers, file servers, Web servers, e-mail servers, print servers). "Typically, servers perform database management, information retrieval, and transaction processing tasks, while clients handle the user interface and input/output operations " (Saffady 1999, 110). In other words, servers deliver access to files, applications, and network communications. Clients handle screen formatting, display of results, and input/output related to specific tasks.

The client/server architecture differs from the traditional file server design model. In the file server model, when a patron issues a request from an OPAC computer, for example, the entire database file is downloaded to the computer making the request. In the client/server model, the database stays on the application server. The client makes the request and sends it to the application server. The server searches for the requested information in its database, finds the relevant information, and sends the results to the client's OPAC. In addition, each client that is connected to the server must have part of the automation software loaded onto its hard disk (e.g., the interface) that allows it to perform some application tasks. User access to the Web for information retrieval, for example, is a client/server architecture.

The client/server architecture uses the Transmission Control Protocol/Internet Protocol (TCP/IP) to establish communications between servers and clients. In the library environment, the Z39.50 protocol is employed in addition to the TCP/IP to facilitate sharing information between clients and servers over the Web (Boss 1997). The main purpose of the Z39.50 protocol is to link heterogeneous automated systems on the Web so that users can access them independent of the automation software or platform they have in place (Macintosh or PC).

In a client/server architecture, servers may be Unix-based minicomputers, high-end microcomputers that operate on Windows NT, or mainframe computers. Clients are usually Windows-based microcomputers, but they can also be Macintosh computers. A client/server architecture may comprise one or more file servers that are connected to multiple clients.

## Types of Client/Server Architecture

There are three main types of client/server architecture: two-tier, three-tier, and thin clients.

### *Two-Tier*

In this design, the application logic is run on the user's client. Clients are desktop computers. They are also known as "fat" or "thick" clients because they have processing capabilities and perform some application tasks. The client's application runs the code that displays the output to the user. The database management system resides in the server. The database processing tasks are done in the server, whereas the application processing tasks (e.g., data manipulation, screen formatting, input/output) are done in the client. When the client issues commands (requests), the database management system in the server searches for the requested information and submits it to the client. Because less information will be transmitted over the network (i.e., only the results of the request), this communication results in faster data transmission between the client and the server. The desktops used as clients are called "fat" or "thick" clients. Two-tier systems are less scalable than three-tier systems, making them unable to support high-volume transactions (Ralston, Reilly, and Hemmendinger 2000).

## *Three-Tier*

In this design, part of the application logic is run in the client (the interface) and another part is run in the server. Clients are desktop computers. They are also referred to as "fat" or "thick" clients because they have processing capabilities and perform some application tasks. A software component called "middleware" is added (Beiser 1999). This component may reside on the database server or on a different server. The three-tier system is used to accommodate high-volume transactions. Having additional servers will speed data transmission over a network. Three-tier systems may be the choice for a WAN environment, whereas two-tier systems are more suitable to run over a LAN.

## *Thin Clients*

Thin clients are computer terminals (rather than desktop computers) that do little or no data processing. The client processes only keyboard input and screen output. All application processing tasks are done in the server. Thin clients are used in a client/server environment to lower the cost of PCs or Macs used in a network. One can combine thin clients with a "thick" or "fat" client in a network. Thin clients may be used as e-mail stations, Web access stations, and/or OPAC stations, for example, whereas "thick" or "fat" clients may be utilized for access and use of application software, such as word processing, home page development, and other tasks that require use of hard disk storage.

# Benefits of a Client/Server Architecture

Client/server architecture is inherently scaleable; that is, it accommodates small and large applications. As Haley (1998) notes, "client/server systems are scalable, so that very large to very small library system implementations can be configured using the same software and by adding more server power" (12). Additional benefits include the following:

- Clients and servers may operate on different computer platforms (PCs and Macs).

- Clients and servers are independent of the underlying network structure (e.g., Ethernet, token ring).

- A client may connect to one or more servers (e.g., an OPAC server, a Web server, an e-mail server).

- A server may connect to multiple clients concurrently.

- Because the Graphical User Interface (GUI) software resides on a client's computer, it allows the client to handle the input/output, data manipulation tasks, and reformatting of screen displays. This shared processing between the client and the server results in increased performance over the network due to reductions in network traffic and the number of tasks managed by the server.

- The sooner the updates of the automation software are installed on servers and clients, the faster users can have access to items added to the collection.

- Users may access the OPAC from remote locations provided their client computers are equipped with a modem. Users must have an Internet service provider to be able to access OPACs remotely.

- Users can share computer peripherals (e.g., printers), which results in cost savings on hardware.

Although the advantages of a client/server architecture are many, there are disadvantages:

- The greatest disadvantage concerns the client software that must be installed and updated on each client's computer in a network (Beiser 1999; Boss 1998). Although installation and updates of the client software in a LAN environment may be time-consuming, they can be a "nightmare" in a WAN environment. This is because the client software must be installed and updated on all client computers that are in the network.

- Failure of a server can render a client/server system unavailable. In addition, if the network fails, all servers in the network become unreachable. Moreover, if one client in a network produces a high volume of requests, all clients in the network may have long response time (Ralston, Reilly, and Hemmendinger 2000). Downtime hampers access to the collection and may cause frustration on the part of the users and staff. It also detracts from the efficiency that is supposed to be achieved through automation.

- The speed and quality of data transmission in a LAN or WAN environment depends on the type of network cables used (e.g., coaxial, twisted pair, fiber optics), the network architecture (e.g., Ethernet, token ring, fiber distributed data interface [FDDI]) in place, and the design used (two-tier, three-tier, or thin client).

- Remote access to the OPAC is delayed when telephone lines are occupied, which may distress users. Denial of access not only frustrates users but also interferes with the efficiency that automation is supposed to introduce.

- Generally, the hardware and software needed for a LAN or WAN are more costly than those needed for the stand-alone configuration. Networking computers with the servers is very expensive, because it requires high-end servers, a licensing fee, and a networking card for each client, among other things. A client/server system is expensive to implement, operate, and maintain (Saffady 1999).

- Maintenance and troubleshooting of a client/server system require knowledge of and skills in computer networking. Media specialists and information professionals who lack this knowledge must rely on experienced personnel, either experienced staff or outside consultants. One problem with using staff in this capacity is that other demands on the staff person's time may take precedence over the needs of the media center or library. Of course, the problem with using outside experts is cost.

For additional information about networking, see Chapter 7.

# SUMMARY

Microcomputers are the systems typically used in media centers and small libraries. Powerful microcomputers have similar power to miniframes and mainframes.

There are two main configuration options for hardware: non-networked and networked. Media specialists and information professionals should evaluate the strengths and weaknesses of each option vis-à-vis the needs of their media centers or libraries. In the networked environment, a media center or library may have a LAN or can be part of a WAN. In either case, the automation software used will most likely be written for a client/server architecture.

Generally speaking, a stand-alone configuration may be the best choice for a media center or library with three to five computer stations where networking is unaffordable. In a networked environment, there are three main design considerations for client/server systems: two-tier, three-tier, and thin clients. A two-tier client/server system is usually preferred for small volume transactions when, for example, two servers and two dozen computer clients exist in a LAN. A three-tier client/server system is the best choice for high-volume transactions where multiple servers and several computer clients are connected to the servers. Thin clients are used when desktop computers are unaffordable. The benefits of the client/server architecture outweigh its drawbacks. Media specialists and information professionals should evaluate the appropriateness of each design based on the needs of their institutions and the cost of implementing a specific design.

# REFERENCES

Beiser, Karl. 1999. Integrated library system software for smaller libraries. Part 2. School, academic, and public libraries. *Library Technology Reports* 35 (4): 365-95.

Boss, Richard. 1997. *The library administrator's automation handbook*. Medford, NJ: Information Today.

————. 1998. Model technology plans for libraries. *Library Technology Reports* 34 (1): 9-109.

Haley, Leigh Watson. 1998. *Library systems: Current developments and future directions*. Washington, DC: Council on Library and Information Resources.

Ralston, Anthony, Edwin D. Reilly, and David Hemmendinger (Eds.). 2000. *Encyclopedia of computer science*. London: Nature Publishing.

Saffady, William. 1999. *Introduction to computers for librarians*. Chicago: American Library Association.

White, Ron. 2002. *How computers work*. Indianapolis, IN: Que.

## *Activity: Hardware Configuration*

**Objective:** To examine the hardware configurations of an automated system used in a media center or small library.

**Description:**

1. Select a media center or a small library that has an automated system. Meet with either the media specialist or information professional, technology coordinator or specialist, or other qualified personnel. Gather information about the hardware configurations, including the

    Type of configuration used (e.g., stand-alone, LAN-based with client/server system, WAN-based with client/server system);

    Number of existing clients;

    Number and name of existing servers (application server, Web server, e-mail server, etc.);

    Type of platform used (i.e., Macintosh or PC);

    Type of network operating system used (e.g., Windows NT, Unix);

    Name of automation software and the modules implemented;

    Cost of the automation software;

    Cost of the hardware configuration;

    Reasons for selecting the existing configuration; and

    Benefits and drawbacks of the exiting configuration.

2. Write a report describing the mission of the media center or small library, the number of patrons it serves, and the size of its collection. Also describe the strengths and weaknesses of the existing configuration from the media specialist or information professional or other qualified person's perspective. Describe the configuration you would choose or the modifications you would make to the existing configuration to best meet the media center's or library's mission and serve its patrons. Justify your answer.

# Chapter 4

---

## System Selection

---

The rapid advancement of computer technology has had a marked impact on the development of automation software. An automated system is no longer a replica of the card catalog; instead it offers colossal features the card catalog could never provide. As additional advances are made, future automated systems will offer even more and better features. For this reason, automation software must be supported by a company that is committed to enhancing the software on a regular basis. Hence, knowledge of a company's history, stability, experiences in automation, quality, and future directions in developing the software are key criteria for selecting an automated system. This is, of course, in addition to the capabilities of the automation software itself.

This chapter covers essential steps in selecting an integrated microcomputer-based automation system and reveals pitfalls to avoid during the selection process.

## THE SELECTION PROCESS

The first step in selecting a microcomputer-based automated system is re-examination of the needs assessment conducted during the preparation process. Review your priority needs, staff needs, user information needs, and budget so that you are able to translate these needs into software features that are essential and desirable in an automated system.

### Select Six Packages

The knowledge about the automation process that you acquired during the preparation process and your review of the literature should assist you in identifying the automated software to consider. Begin by reading the latest two issues of *Library Journal*. This publication also has an annual survey of selected automation companies titled "Automation System Marketplace" that appears on April 1. In this survey, you will find a brief profile of each of the automation companies and the software packages they offer. The survey also includes tables and charts that show the companies' sales to different types of libraries inside and outside the United States. It also describes the trends and developments in library automation. *Library Journal* is available on the Web at http://www.libraryjournal.reviewsnews.com. From the tables and charts provided, identify the software packages that are suitable for your type of library and read the profiles of their respective companies. *Library Journal* also publishes the "InfoTech" column in each of its issues, which provides the latest information about technology developments, including automation products.

Next, consult the latest issues of *Library Technology Reports* containing reviews about the software packages under consideration. This publication provides comprehensive reviews of various products and technologies suitable for all types of libraries. Take notes about the strengths and weaknesses of each module. Note that system selection should not be based on reviews only; your testing and evaluation of the packages to determine their suitability for your needs and requirements is also important.

Preview each package yourself. Request an interactive demonstration diskette from each vendor, but be aware that the demonstrations on such diskettes may be incomplete. For more complete, interactive demonstrations, visit media centers or libraries that have recently implemented each system you are considering. This will allow you to experiment with many applications online and also to see how well the software operates in real situations.

Invite a sales representative from each of the six software companies to demonstrate the software in-house. If you invited company representatives to discuss their software during the preparation process, invite them again, because by this time you have gained more knowledge about automation and are better prepared to ask more specific and in-depth questions. Using the notes from your reading and software previews, prepare a list of questions to ask each representative. Demonstrations provided by representatives usually reflect the latest software enhancements, thus giving you up-to-date information that has not yet appeared in the literature. You may want to develop a table of features for the six packages you preview. Such a table will allow you to compare the systems under consideration at a glance.

## Narrow Your Choices

Compile and examine all your notes from initial knowledge acquisitions, later readings, previews, and demonstrations to screen the six software choices now before you. Add features you have found in the reviews, demonstrations, and from using the software packages at neighborhood libraries to the table you have developed. This table will help you to self-rate these software packages and to identify the packages that provide most of the essential and desirable features you seek. Using all the information you have gathered, narrow your choices to three software packages that best meet your needs and priorities. Remember to consult with members of the automation advisory committee for their input. In narrowing your choices, consider the following aspects:

> The features that match your needs;
>
> The capability to integrate multiple modules;
>
> The presence of all modules needed;
>
> The presence of essential features in each module;

The strengths of each module;

The overall software capabilities (e.g., for multi-user access, Web access, networking, expandability);

Compliance with the latest bibliographic standards (i.e., MARC 21) and the information retrieval standard Z39.50;

The architecture supported (e.g., client/server);

The software vendor's plan for providing new applications;

The frequency of software updates;

The quality of service provided by the software company (e.g., technical support, turnaround time for assistance) and the hours that service is available;

The software documentation and its organization;

The type and cost of training provided; and

The cost of the software, software updates, and annual maintenance support.

## Develop a Request for Proposal

After you have narrowed your list of software choices to three packages, subject these three packages to detailed comparison and evaluation. To do this, develop a request for proposal (RFP) based on the needs assessment, your notes, the table of features you developed, checklists or sample RFPs supplied by software companies, RFPs developed by media centers and libraries that have implemented automation, RFPs included in the literature (like the one in this chapter), and consultation with colleagues.

Why develop an RFP? An RFP provides means for comparing and evaluating various systems and for selecting a system that best suits your needs. Developing an RFP is one of the most important steps in procuring an automated system. Even when an RFP is not required, it is a useful part of the procurement process because it forces you to determine your automation needs (Day, Flanders, and Zuck 1994; Boss 1998). An RFP may be more than a guide for comparison, however; it may result in a binding agreement between a media center or library and a vendor, which stipulates the specifications an automated system must meet (Meghabghab 1994).

Many software vendors supply customers with their own sample RFPs or checklists. However, companies' RFPs, although useful, contain specifications that are tailored to their own systems. Regardless of how well a vendor's RFP is developed, it is recommended that you develop your own.

## Preparing the Request for Proposal

Preparing an RFP requires knowledge of an automated system's functional specifications so that one is able to respond to a vendor's questions and explain the specifications described. Although RFPs may vary in format, certain things are essential. These are consistency of organization, use of appropriate verbs, specificity of the specifications, and a good writing style. A sample RFP appears at the end of this chapter. Following are suggestions for writing an RFP:

- Organize the RFP into sections, including separate sections devoted to each module.

- Use the word *must* to indicate the essential specifications and the word *should* to indicate desirable or preferred specifications. *Essential specifications* are those you cannot do without; *desirable* or *preferred specifications* are nice to have, but you can do without them.

- List the tasks the system should perform, rather than how it should do them.

- Include specifications for all modules desired in a system.

- Describe specifications the system must incorporate at present and in the near future.

- Define all of the codes, symbols, descriptors, and scales you use, and give vendors instructions about how to apply them.

- Use the following verbs: *allow, display, design, perform, provide, detect, initiate, generate, search, calculate, maintain, can, capable of, prompt,* and the like, as applicable.

- When the vendor is asked to rate the software's ability to meet specifications using a scale (e.g., 1–5 or 1–10), ask the vendor to explain any below-average ratings.

- Allow sufficient space at the end of each section for the vendor's response or comments.

- Request a copy of the company's latest audited financial statement. Also request the names of media centers or libraries (especially those in your state) that have implemented the software. Ask for the names of key personnel and a market survey of studies about the system. This information is essential for evaluating the company's stability and the qualifications of its key personnel, especially those in the technical support and processing units.

- Allow vendors four to six weeks to respond to the RFP.

## Organizing the RFP

The first page of the RFP includes a cover sheet with the title of the RFP, the name of the person to whom it is submitted, the company name and address, the name and address of the contact person in the media center or library, and the submission date. The second page is a table of contents. The pages that follow it may include six main sections in the following order:

Instructions to the vendor

Introduction to the media center or library

Software specifications (both essential and preferred)

Hardware specifications

Request for price quotation

Notice of intent to respond

## Instructions to the Vendor

This section explains the organization of the RFP. It defines the descriptors (e.g., essential and preferred), rating system or scale (e.g., 1-5 or 1-10), and codes (e.g., A= Available, N= Not available, U= Under development, F= Future development) used.

## Introduction to the Media Center or Library

This section provides brief background information about the media center or library, its goals and objectives, and how these goals and objectives relate to automation. Reports based on the data gathered during the planning process may be included.

## Software Specifications

This section lists the essential and preferred specifications for each module of the automated system. This is the heart of the RFP. For an example of software specifications, see Figures 4.1 to 4.8 at the end of this chapter.

## Hardware Specifications

This section provides specifications for the essential hardware, that is, hardware that is required to support the automation system. In some cases, one vendor provides both the hardware and the software needed for the automated system. In other cases, the software vendor does not supply the needed hardware. If this is the case for any of the software packages you are considering, then you must develop a separate RFP for the needed hardware.

Hardware includes database and other servers, client computers, printer(s), barcode scanner(s), and other hardware or equipment needed to support the operation of the system. (This required hardware depends on what configuration you are planning to use for your automated system. See Chapter 3 for a discussion of common configurations.)

Because hardware specifications change quickly over time, they are not provided in the sample RFP. The preferred method for developing your hardware specifications is to examine the hardware requirements for the automation systems under consideration. It is advised that you purchase hardware that exceeds the minimum specifications required so that the hardware will accommodate future software enhancements and developments. You may want to consult with the automation advisory committee, and especially your technology expert, before writing an RFP or purchasing your hardware. You may also want to contact colleagues who have recently implemented automation systems in their media centers or libraries to obtain their advice about hardware acquisition.

**Note:** Different software packages have different hardware requirements. Some packages run only in networked environments, some run only on certain platforms (PC or Mac). Software vendors usually provide specifications for the hardware required to run their packages. These specifications must be examined before developing the RFP for hardware. Look for them in the vendors' product catalogs.

*Request for Price Quotation*

This section provides a form for the vendor to complete. The form, developed by the RFP writer, may include a description of each item needed and the quantity desired (e.g., system modules, multi-user access, record conversion, barcodes, barcode scanners). The vendor is asked to provide the list price of each item, the applicable discounted prices, the cost of a maintenance contract, the cost of updates and enhancements, and the cost of any other items or features that are important to the operation of the system. It is best to request a 30-day price guarantee (fixed price) for the listed items.

*Notice of Intent to Respond*

The notice of intent to respond is a form included with the RFP. The vendor fills out and returns the form to let the media specialist or information professional know that a response to the submitted RFP is forthcoming. Allow four to six weeks for the vendor to respond.

## Review the RFP and Send It to Vendors

After the RFP is written, have members of the automation committee and one or two outside experts in automation (e.g., a professor of automation at a nearby college or university) or colleagues experienced in automation review it and provide you with feedback. Duplicate and mail the RFP to each of the three software companies under consideration.

## Evaluate Responses to the RFP and Choose One Package

Review the RFPs returned by the designated vendors and evaluate them for a final screening. Select the software package that best meets your essential specifications. If two or three packages are comparable or equal in this respect (which is unlikely), then the determining factors are the quality of service provided by the vendor, the cost of the software, and the annual maintenance cost.

## Contract to Purchase the Software

After selecting one of the software packages, inform your supervisor(s) about your decision to obtain their approval. Contact the respective vendor about your decision. The vendor will send you a contract for purchasing the software. The contract with the vendor must include

A schedule for software delivery, installation, testing, and implementation;

A schedule for training personnel to use the software;

The vendor's promise to deliver a software package that meets the specifications stipulated in the RFP;

The vendor's comments or explanations about certain specifications, ratings of features, and plans for providing enhancements and updates; and

A payment plan. If you are not financing the purchase, consider paying for it in three installations: one-third upon signing the contract, one-third upon successful installation and performance testing, and a final payment upon successful performance over time.

Have your media center's or library's attorney review the contract before you sign it.

## Pitfalls to Avoid

Making mistakes during the selection process is inevitable, especially when a decision is made to automate without adequate time and staff training. Careful preparation, as outlined in Chapter 2, will help you avoid common pitfalls. Nevertheless, sometimes unexpected events—even windfalls—can take media specialists and information professionals by surprise. One day, your supervisor may inform you that money is available to automate your media center or library. You may be asked to make a decision about an automated system within a few days or weeks. Surprised? Do not be! Be prepared to make a wise decision about selecting an automation system. Most important is to avoid some common traps that unwary media specialists or information professionals may fall into. Good planning and awareness of these traps will help you to avoid them. Following are "do not do" and "do" lists for selecting an automation system.

### The Do Not Do List

- Do not assume that cost indicates suitability.

- Do not overemphasize cost in deciding which software package is best.

- Do not eliminate software packages that are slightly more expensive than your budget allows, because they may have better features and the vendors may provide better support.

- Do not be taken in by the charm or educational background or experience of the sales representative or consultant. The sales representative's job is to impress you to sell the product. Focus on the product, not the sales representative.

- Do not purchase a system based solely on the software preview, a colleague's recommendation, or cost. Thoroughly test and evaluate the software packages. Remember to involve the staff in this process.

- Do not select a system without developing your own RFP. If you have been given only a few days or weeks to decide on an automated system, you will most likely not be able to develop an RFP. However, if you have adequate time to plan for the automation project, then you should consider developing an RFP. No "canned" RFP can do justice to the unique requirements of your media center or library. Although time-consuming, creating a customized RFP is essential to ensure that the automation system will meet the unique needs of your media center or library (Beiser 1999a; Beiser 1999b). If necessary, you must convince staff and administration (and yourself) of the need for a customized RFP.

- Do not choose a system before evaluating and comparing vendors' responses to the RFP. Allow adequate time to examine vendors' responses to your RFP.

- Do not select a software package that does not meet 90 percent of your needs and requirements.

## *The Do List (Key Things to Remember)*

- Do your homework before selecting an automation system. Analyze and prioritize your media center's or library's needs, research existing systems, find reviews, consult with colleagues, and preview and test the software packages under consideration.

- Form and involve an automation advisory committee in the planning and selection process.

- Involve staff and users in the planning and selection process. Remember to include your technology coordinator or expert, if you have one.

- Keep a good communication flow between you and all those who will be affected by automation.

- Develop a table of features to compare the software packages under consideration. This table will serve as a basis for drafting your RFP.

- Develop an RFP if you have adequate time for selecting and implementing the automation project.

- Familiarize yourself with emerging technologies and their impact on automation. Consider purchasing an automation system not only for the present but also for the near future (three years). Your software and hardware should be expandable to accommodate future developments and needs.

- Consider purchasing an automated system that is used in a wide area network (WAN) in a specific area or district. You will gain many benefits from such a venture, including access to a richer collection, saving time processing library materials, and handling interlibrary loan requests online.

# SUMMARY

Selecting an automated system is a time-consuming task that takes a long-term commitment of financial and personnel resources. The selection decision should be based on needs assessment, review of the literature, evaluation, and comparison of existing software packages. Although time-consuming, developing an RFP is highly recommended, even when software packages under consideration are supported by reputable automation companies. An RFP is the best means of articulating the specifications an automated system must and should meet; it allows comparison among various systems and provides justification for selecting a particular system.

Media specialists and information professionals must be involved not only in the selection process but also in the decision about the system procurement, because they are the most knowledgeable personnel about the collection, users' needs and information-seeking behavior, and administrative conditions of their workplace.

# REFERENCES

Beiser, Karl. 1999a. Integrated library system software for smaller libraries. Part 1. Special, academic and public libraries. *Library Technology Reports* 35 (2): 119-262.

————. 1999b. Integrated library system software for smaller libraries. Part 2. School, academic and public libraries. *Library Technology Reports* 35 (4): 365-548.

Boss, Richard W. 1998. Model technology plans for libraries. *Library Technology Reports* 34 (1): 1-109.

Day, Teresa Thurman, Bruce Flanders, and Gregory Zuck. (Eds.) 1994. *Automation for school libraries: How to do it from those who have done it.* Chicago: American Library Association.

Meghabghab, Dania Bilal. 1994. Purchasing a microcomputer-based automated system for school and public libraries: Points to consider and pitfalls to avoid. Proceedings of the Ninth Integrated Online Library Systems Meeting, New York, May, 139-46.

## *Activity: Cost Analysis*

**Objective 1:** To select specific software and conduct a cost analysis.

**Description:** Select an integrated automated system for which you would like to conduct a cost analysis. Perform the following activities:

- Review the latest "Automated Marketplace" article that appears in the April 1 issue of *Library Journal*. Select one software package that is suitable for your media center or library and determine the module you will be needing.

- Identify the modules you need and the cost. Identify whether the software is for a single user or multi-user access. Describe whether the software is for a stand-alone configuration or a networked configuration.

- Include the cost of personnel training, technical support, and updates.

- Calculate the total cost.

**Objective 2:** To select hardware compatible with the software and perform a cost analysis.

**Description:** Identify the hardware needed to support the operation of the automation software chosen in Objective 1. Perform the following activities:

- Provide the quantity, item description, and item cost for the following: a file server, printer(s), lookup stations, inventory device(s), barcode scanner(s), uninterruptible power supply unit (UPS), networking operating system, networking cards, maintenance, and other hardware pieces recommended by the vendor.

- Calculate the cost of the hardware.

- Calculate the total cost of software and hardware.

- Provide the Web site address of the vendor you contacted for the software and hardware. Include a copy of the materials from which you obtained the descriptions of the items/products and the costs.

- Describe briefly your experience with this activity.

# SAMPLE REQUEST FOR PROPOSAL

Figures 4.1 through 4.8 list the minimum essential specifications for a Windows-based integrated automated system that supports utilities, cataloging, authority control, the OPAC, circulation, acquisitions, and serials.

The specifications provided in these examples may be modified to meet the specific needs and requirements of individual media centers and libraries. Because only minimum essential specifications are listed in the examples, preferred specifications should be added. On the other hand, a number of the specifications considered essential in this RFP may be merely preferred specifications for a particular media center or library.

The sample RFP applies a numbering system to identify each feature described, as well as a scale and a code for the vendor to use in responding. To complete this type of RFP, the vendor writes the appropriate scale or code in the box next to the feature being described. At the end of each section of the specification list, additional space is provided for vendor comments. Vendors are instructed to refer to features by their identifying numbers when discussing them. Staff who prepare the RFP for their individual media center or library may modify the numbering system, as well as the scale and code used, based on preference and ease of use.

The sample RFP offered in this section is based on the author's lengthy experience in library automation, consultation with practitioners, examination and evaluation of well-developed RFPs, and sources in the literature.

## Figure 4.1. General essential specifications.

| Codes for Column 3: | A = Available | Scale for Column 4   1-5: |
|---|---|---|
| | N = Not available | 1 = Very poor |
| | U = Under development | 5 = Excellent |
| | F = Future development | |

**Note:** The term *must* means essential.

| Feature Number | The system must: | Code: A-N-U-F | Scale: 1-5 |
|---|---|---|---|
| G-1 | support OPAC, circulation, cataloging, acquisitions, serials, utilities, MARC 21, inventory, and authority control in one fully integrated system. | | |
| G-2 | allow modules in G-1 to share one common database and to work both independently of and concurrently with each other. | | |
| G-3 | support a Graphical User Interface (GUI) in all the modules. | | |
| G-4 | be networkable, and support Windows NT operating system for server. | | |
| G-5 | support Windows 98 (or higher) operating system for client computers. | | |
| G-6 | support TCP/IP Internet protocol for communications between clients and servers in a Local Area Network (LAN). | | |
| G-7 | have a client/server architecture with two-tier and three-tier design. | | |
| G-8 | provide a Web OPAC and allow its access remotely via a Web browser. | | |
| G-9 | be compatible with the Z39.50 standards for clients and servers. | | |
| G-10 | have a database management system (DBMS), such as FairCom or Oracle. Please specify your DBMS. | | |
| G-11 | allow authorized staff to login from any client computer station in the LAN. | | |
| G-12 | accommodate simultaneous multi-user access of 100 existing computer stations and simultaneous multi-user access of a minimum of 200 stations in the near future. | | |

**Figure 4.1 (Continued)**

| Feature Number | The system must: | Code: A-N-U-F | Scale: 1-5 |
|---|---|---|---|
| G-13 | accommodate a patron database of 50,000 and support its future growth to a minimum of 150,000. | | |
| G-14 | accommodate an existing collection size of 150,000 titles and support its future growth to 300,000. | | |
| G-15 | be compatible with brief and full U.S. MARC/MARC 21. | | |
| G-16 | allow import and export of U.S. MARC/MARC 21 records. | | |
| G-17 | store, display, read, input, and output information in brief and full U.S. MARC/MARC 21 formats. | | |
| G-18 | support multi-user access to Web OPAC for a minimum of 100 users. | | |
| G-19 | allow program data backup while users are on the system. | | |
| G-20 | support nonproprietary, industry-standard barcode labels of at least 14 digits, and optical scanning devices (e.g., light pens, wands, laser guns, etc.). | | |
| G-21 | support the collection inventory using a portable barcode reader/scanner/laser gun. | | |
| G-22 | contain a utilities or equivalent module for rebuilding database files, rebuilding keywords, checking database integrity, reloading database files, and the like tasks. | | |
| G-23 | provide authority control based on MARC 21 for: Author. Title. Subject. Series. | | |
| G-24 | maintain a context-sensitive help and/or a help index for all screens. | | |
| G-25 | contain a multilayered security feature with passwords that allow staff to change passwords | | |

| Feature Number | The system must: | Code: A-N-U-F | Scale: 1-5 |
|---|---|---|---|
| G-26 | alert for backup before exiting. | | |
| G-27 | prevent unauthorized access of the software. | | |
| G-28 | allow deletion of files and/or records. | | |
| G-29 | alert for deletion of files and/or records. | | |
| G-30 | confirm deletion of files and/or records. | | |
| G-31 | be: | | |
| | user friendly. | | |
| | easy for staff and patrons to use. | | |
| | equipped with easy and advanced search interfaces. | | |
| | equipped with meaningful icons that represent functions. | | |
| | equipped with attractive and uncluttered screen | | |
| | interfaces. | | |
| G-32 | support the issue of interlibrary loan requests online. | | |
| G-33 | support an online union catalog of bibliographic records that can be shared in wide area network (WAN). | | |
| G-34 | be expandable to accommodate future applications. | | |
| G-35 | integrate imported Web sites into the MARC database. | | |
| G-36 | provide a cataloging module for Web sites. | | |
| G-37 | allow the export of Web sites from the MARC database. | | |
| G-38 | support use of commercial Web browser, including but not limited to Netscape and Microsoft Windows Internet Explorer. | | |
| G-39 | automatically launch Web sites from OPAC by clicking on them and without closing the connection of the OPAC. | | |

**Figure 4.1 (Continued)**

| Feature Number | The system must: | Code A-N-U-F | Scale: 1-5 |
|---|---|---|---|
| G-40 | provide a repeatable 856 field (a minimum of 5 per record) in a MARC record. | | |
| G-41 | place each of the imported Web sites in a separate 856 MARC field. | | |
| G-42 | generate a variety of statistics and other re-ports and allow staff to customize reports. (Please supply sample of predefined reports). | | |
| G-43 | interface with bibliographic utilities, includ-ing but not limited to the Online Computer Library Center (OCLC). | | |
| G-44 | allow the import of MARC records from bib-liographic utilities into the local database. | | |
| G-45 | provide multi-tasking and allow the screen of one module to remain active while working in another module. | | |
| G-46 | provide point and click navigation using a mouse. | | |
| G-47 | have a fast response time, especially in a LAN environment. Please specify the response time for the following functions supported by (**X**) microprocessor with a clock speed of (**X**) MHz: | | |
| | saving a cataloged record in a full U.S. MARC/MARC 21 format. | | |
| | downloading 50 U.S. MARC/MARC 21 records from a floppy diskette or other medium. | | |
| | filing 50 newly cataloged or downloaded records. | | |
| | building keywords for 50 newly downloaded records. | | |
| | building 50 newly created cross references. | | |
| | searching by two keywords with the Boolean operator OR in OPAC. | | |
| | searching by two keywords with the Boolean operator AND in OPAC. | | |
| | searching by two keywords with the Boolean operator NOT in OPAC. | | |
| | searching with nested logic using more than three Boolean operators. | | |

| Feature Number | The system must: | Code: A-N-U-F | Scale: 1-5 |
|---|---|---|---|
| G-47 | include a screen saver, with time out adjustable by staff. | | |
| G-48 | allow printing to a screen and a printer. | | |
| G-49 | allow full editing of data in all modules. | | |
| G-50 | allow patrons to access the OPAC module only and without a password. | | |
| | **The vendor must:** | | |
| G-51 | provide technical support through a toll-free telephone number between the hours of 7 a.m. and 6 p.m. Eastern Standard Time with response to calls within one hour. | | |
| G-52 | be able to dial into the media center/library's file/database servers via a modem to diagnose and troubleshoot problems. | | |
| G-53 | be able to communicate by e-mail. | | |
| G-54 | provide frequent updates and enhancements of the software at no additional charge. | | |
| G-55 | provide on-site training in system use. | | |
| G-56 | supply a full set of print documentation upon system installation. | | |
| G-57 | maintain clear, well-written, well-organized, and easy-to-use documentation. The documentation must have tabs with headings, explain the operation of the entire system, and provide instructions with examples and illustrations for each module. It must also be easy to update and include both a glossary and an alphabetical index. | | |
| G-58 | have qualified, well-trained, and friendly technical support and technical processing staff. | | |

**X** = to be filled by media specialists/information professionals.

**This space is provided for vendor comments and explanation.**
**Please use additional sheets if needed. Refer to features by the feature number (column 1).**

## Figure 4.2. Essential specifications for utilities.

Codes for Column 3:   A = Available
                      N = Not available
                      U = Under development
                      F = Future development

Scale for Column 4   1-5:
    1 = Very poor
    5 = Excellent

**Note:** The term *must* means essential.

| Feature Number | The system must: | Code: A-N-U-F | Scale: 1-5 |
|---|---|---|---|
| U-1 | support full system backup. | A-N-U-F | |
| U-2 | diagnose and repair database problems. | A-N-U-F | |
| U-3 | build keyword indexes. | A-N-U-F | |
| U-4 | rebuild keyword indexes. | A-N-U-F | |
| U-5 | build author, title, and subject indexes. | A-N-U-F | |
| U-6 | rebuild author, title, and subject indexes. | A-N-U-F | |
| U-7 | build MARC headings for: | | |
| | Author | A-N-U-F | |
| | Title | A-N-U-F | |
| | Subject | A-N-U-F | |
| | Series | A-N-U-F | |
| | Authority | A-N-U-F | |
| | Call number | A-N-U-F | |
| | Material category | A-N-U-F | |
| | Other, please indicate | A-N-U-F | |
| U-8 | rebuild MARC headings for: | | |
| | Author | A-N-U-F | |
| | Title | A-N-U-F | |
| | Subject | A-N-U-F | |
| | Series | A-N-U-F | |
| | Authority | A-N-U-F | |
| | Call number | A-N-U-F | |
| | Material category | A-N-U-F | |
| | Other, please indicate. | | |
| U-9 | build/rebuild MARC headings for selected files as specified. | A-N-U-F | |

| Feature Number | The system must: | Code: A-N-U-F | Scale: 1-5 |
|---|---|---|---|
| U-10 | provide backup for: | | |
| | acquisitions files | A-N-U-F | |
| | cataloging files | A-N-U-F | |
| | circulation files | A-N-U-F | |
| | interlibrary loan files | A-N-U-F | |
| | inventory data files | A-N-U-F | |
| | patron files | A-N-U-F | |
| | serials files | A-N-U-F | |
| | other files, please indicate. | | |
| U-11 | record errors as it rebuilds database files. | A-N-U-F | |
| U-12 | restore backup files as needed. | A-N-U-F | |
| U-13 | support setting keywords to be indexed based on MARC tags. | A-N-U-F | |
| U-14 | activate/deactivate specific keywords. | A-N-U-F | |
| U-15 | build/rebuild authority records. | A-N-U-F | |
| U-16 | update keywords as new MARC records are downloaded or added into the database. | A-N-U-F | |
| U-17 | empty the keyword index as needed and re-generate the index for the database. | A-N-U-F | |
| U-18 | empty all index files and regenerate them as needed. | A-N-U-F | |
| U-19 | support global deletion of material messages. | A-N-U-F | |
| U-20 | enable creation of user-defined indexes for: | | |
| | material records (author, title, call number, etc.) and | A-N-U-F | |
| | patron records (name, address, barcode, etc.). | A-N-U-F | |
| U-21 | provide a password protection. | A-N-U-F | |
| U-22 | set up backup date and time. | A-N-U-F | |
| U-23 | support ease of navigation among the differ-ent components. | A-N-U-F | |
| U-24 | provide a pull-down menu under each com-ponent. | A-N-U-F | |
| U-25 | provide a glossary. | A-N-U-F | |

## Figure 4.2 (Continued)

| Feature Number | The system must: | Code: A-N-U-F | Scale: 1-5 |
|---|---|---|---|
| U-26 | support setting up multi-level passwords. | A-N-U-F | |
| U-27 | enable setting up material and patron barcodes. | A-N-U-F | |
| U-28 | allow addition and deletion of material and patron barcodes. | A-N-U-F | |
| U-29 | allow editing of material and patron barcodes. | A-N-U-F | |
| U-30 | support setting up the media center's or library's site information. | A-N-U-F | |
| U-31 | enable identification and set up of printers. | A-N-U-F | |
| U-32 | allow set up of modem type and baud rate. | A-N-U-F | |
| U-33 | diagnose installation problems and provide means for remediation. | A-N-U-F | |
| U-34 | support setting up and editing the calendar. | A-N-U-F | |
| U-35 | save all files, reports, and statistics. | A-N-U-F | |
| U-36 | print selected and/or all database files. | A-N-U-F | |
| U-37 | permit setting backup date and time. | A-N-U-F | |
| U-38 | provide online guidance in installing the software. | A-N-U-F | |

This space is provided for vendor comments and explanation.
Please use additional sheets if needed.  Refer to features by the feature number (column 1).

## Figure 4.3. Essential specifications for cataloging.

Codes for Column 3:   A = Available
                      N = Not available
                      U = Under development
                      F = Future development

Scale for Column 4   1-5:
                     1 = Very poor
                     5 = Excellent

**Note:** The term *must* means essential.

| Feature Number | The system must: | Code: A-N-U-F | Scale: 1-5 |
|---|---|---|---|
| C-1 | be Windows-based with a GUI interface. | | |
| C-2 | allow entry using a mouse and a keyboard. | | |
| C-3 | have a separate module for cataloging. | | |
| C-4 | function independently from other modules. | | |
| C-5 | function concurrently with other modules. | | |
| C-6 | support cataloging in real time (e.g., online). | | |
| C-7 | file newly cataloged or downloaded records in real time. | | |
| C-8 | construct indexes automatically and make them available for access immediately after filing. | | |
| C-9 | provide ease of movement among modules without re-login and through point and click using a mouse. | | |
| C-10 | support:<br><br>AACR2R.<br><br>All MARC designators (e.g., the Leader, the fixed field, variable data fields, and tags from 000 to 900).<br><br>Brief and full U.S. MARC/MARC 21 standard.<br><br>ISBD. | | |
| C-11 | allow the import of MARC records into the local cataloging database directly from the Web. | | |
| C-12 | provide a separate module for cataloging Web sites. | | |
| C-13 | integrate newly cataloged Web sites with the cataloging database. | | |

**Figure 4.3 (Continued)**

| Feature Number | The system must: | Code: A-N-U-F | Scale: 1-5 |
|---|---|---|---|
| C-14 | label cataloged Web sites when they appear in the OPAC. | | |
| C-15 | allow truncation and wild-character searching. | | |
| C-16 | maintain a single master bibliographic record with item records attached to it. | | |
| C-17 | provide error detection, especially before filing new records. | | |
| C-18 | allow members in an online union catalog to retain their own holdings and shelf location. | | |
| C-19 | permit global update, editing, and deletion of existing and imported records. | | |
| C-20 | support backup for the database and all files in the system. | | |
| C-21 | create item records for circulation automatically, based on cataloged and downloaded records. | | |
| C-22 | allow addition of a copy of a record to support multiple copies and multivolume items. | | |
| C-23 | support addition of barcodes for multiple copies and multivolume items. | | |
| C-24 | provide online flexible editing capabilities that do not require going from a data entry mode to an editing mode. Editing must be supported for any data field without retyping the entire line or data field. | | |
| C-25 | transfer changes in the union catalog to local sites and vice versa. | | |
| C-26 | support merging records from commercial vendors with locally created records in order to provide full records for an online union catalog. | | |
| C-27 | support merging records from commercial vendors with locally created records in order to provide full records for an online union catalog. | | |

| Feature Number | The system must: | Code: A-N-U-F | Scale: 1-5 |
|---|---|---|---|
| C-28 | allow staff to turn on and off certain features, including but not limited to saving a record without input in MARC tags 100 to 500. | | |
| C-29 | support the display of a cataloged record on the screen before printing. | | |
| C-30 | provide an alert for record deletion if the circulation transaction is active on copies. | | |
| C-31 | customize and generate lists with fields and headings defined by staff to include, but not limited to:<br><br>A printed catalog of books. | | |
| | A separate printed catalog of audiovisual materials for each media center and for all media centers in a union catalog. | | |
| | New titles added, etc. for each media center and all media centers in a union catalog. | | |
| | serials. | | |
| C-32 | disallow deletion of records if any copies remain attached to a record. | | |
| C-33 | update all appropriate index entries automatically as changes are made in item and copy records, or as these records are deleted from the database. | | |
| C-34 | support Dewey Decimal Classification call numbers. | | |
| C-35 | support *Sears* and *Library of Congress List of Subject Headings*. | | |
| C-36 | allow manual keying of records and:<br><br>Addition of diacritical marks. | | |
| | Addition and deletion of subfields. | | |
| | Addition and deletion of tags. | | |
| C-37 | define each element in the Leader and fixed field of the MARC record in a pop-up window, pull-down menu format, or in a labeled format as the cursor is pointed at an element. | | |

**Figure 4.3 (Continued)**

| Feature Number | The system must: | Code: A-N-U-F | Scale: 1-5 |
|---|---|---|---|
| C-38 | provide an end-of-the line word wrapping feature to avoid sentence truncation. | | |
| C-39 | allow the title of a previously cataloged record to be copied for a new title edition, software version, etc. | | |
| C-40 | display records in a card catalog format in OPAC. | | |
| C-41 | support complete database maintenance and generate reports to include, but not limited to: | | |
| | new titles. | | |
| | titles with duplicate ISBN, ISSN and/or LCCN. | | |
| | titles without ISBN, ISSN, and/or LCCN. | | |
| | updated titles. | | |
| C-42 | provide automatic daily back-up or alert operator to backup before exiting. | | |
| C-43 | support cataloging of a variety of types of materials in a U.S. MARC/MARC 21 format to include, but not limited to: | | |
| | books. | | |
| | CD-ROM. | | |
| | videos. | | |
| | kits. | | |
| | Laserdiscs and DVD. | | |
| | sound recordings (e.g., music CD). | | |
| | other media (please specify). | | |
| C-44 | support setting up the type of materials as default for original cataloging. | | |
| C-45 | generate, save, and print partial and full reports for the following fields: | | |
| | Author. | | |
| | ISBN. | | |
| | Shelflist. | | |
| | Subject. | | |
| | Title. | | |

| Feature Number | The system must: | Code: A-N-U-F | Scale: 1-5 |
|---|---|---|---|
| C-46 | allow printing proof sheets of a MARC record before saving. | | |
| C-47 | provide security through a password protection. | | |
| C-48 | support complete database set up and customization to include, but not limited to: | | |
| | Apply and delete LC classification number. | | |
| | Apply and delete LC subject headings. | | |
| | Apply and delete local subject headings. | | |
| | Apply and delete *Sears* subject headings. | | |
| | Define field tags for brief MARC records. | | |
| | Delete LC classification number. | | |
| | Other (please describe). | | |
| C-49 | allow batch downloading of MARC records from external sources (e.g., *Alliance Plus*, *Bibliofile*, *Precision One*, etc.). | | |
| C-50 | zap imported records with existing records for review. | | |
| C-51 | Display duplicate records for review. | | |
| C-52 | display and print a blank MARC record. | | |
| C-53 | allow the export of MARC records on different media in both brief and full formats by a variety of methods to include: | | |
| | author. | | |
| | barcode. | | |
| | combined features. | | |
| | call number. | | |
| | LCCN. | | |
| | subject. | | |
| | title. | | |
| C-54 | support large field sizes for data entry to avoid record truncation. Please specify the maximum length of a variable data field allowed in a MARC record. | | |

**Figure 4.3 (Continued)**

| Feature Number | The system must: | Code:<br>A-N-U-F | Scale:<br>1-5 |
|---|---|---|---|
| C-55 | allow selection of MARC fields for key-word indexing. | | |
| C-56 | label each tag in a MARC record. | | |
| C-57 | display and print a blank MARC record. | | |
| C-58 | allow fields to be locally defined (e.g., 900 for local call number). | | |
| C-59 | allow addition of the following information to each MARC record: | | |
| | Acquisition. | | |
| | Barcode. | | |
| | Copy and volume number. | | |
| | Fund. | | |
| | Price. | | |
| | Vendor name. | | |
| | Other information (please describe). | | |
| C-60 | support searching by: | | |
| | Author. | | |
| | Title. | | |
| | Subject. | | |
| | Keyword (from author, title, subject, series, and notes fields). | | |
| | Boolean operators (AND, OR, NOT). | | |
| | ISBN. | | |
| | ISSN. | | |
| | LCCN. | | |
| | Material type | | |
| | Other (please specify). | | |

This space is provided for vendor comments and explanation.
Please use additional sheets if needed. Refer to features by the feature number (column 1).

## Figure 4.4. Essential specifications for authority control.

Codes for Column 3: A = Available          Scale for Column 4   1-5:
                    N = Not available              1 = Very poor
                    U = Under development          5 = Excellent
                    F = Future development

**Note:** The term *must* means essential.

| Feature Number | The system must: | Code: A-N-U-F | Scale: 1-5 |
|---|---|---|---|
| A-1 | be Windows-based with a GUI interface. | A-N-U-F | |
| A-2 | interface with cataloging and OPAC. | A-N-U-F | |
| A-3 | function independently from other modules. | A-N-U-F | |
| A-4 | provide a separate module for authority control that conforms to U.S. MARC/MARC 21. | A-N-U-F | |
| A-5 | support authority control for: | | |
| | author. | A-N-U-F | |
| | series. | A-N-U-F | |
| | subject. | A-N-U-F | |
| | title. | A-N-U-F | |
| A-6 | protect against the deletion of authorities that are still attached to bibliographic records. | A-N-U-F | |
| A-7 | allow online maintenance of all fields in individual authority records. | A-N-U-F | |
| A-8 | support the import of authority records from external sources. | A-N-U-F | |
| A-9 | merges and files imported authority records with existing records. | A-N-U-F | |
| A-10 | flags duplicate authority records and allow their deletion. | A-N-U-F | |
| A-11 | allow creation of authority records online. | A-N-U-F | |
| A-12 | allow editing of authority records online. | A-N-U-F | |
| A-13 | allow deletion of authority records online. | A-N-U-F | |
| A-14 | display problems with matches of headings against authority records when authorities are merged or changed. | A-N-U-F | |

**Figure 4.4 (Continued)**

| Feature Number | The system must: | Code: A-N-U-F | Scale: 1-5 |
|---|---|---|---|
| A-15 | support *see* and *see also* references. | A-N-U-F | |
| A-16 | flag or disallow blind references. | A-N-U-F | |
| A-17 | relink modified authorities to their respective titles. | A-N-U-F | |
| A-18 | allow searching of authority records by: | | |
| | author. | A-N-U-F | |
| | series. | A-N-U-F | |
| | subject. | A-N-U-F | |
| | title. | A-N-U-F | |
| A-19 | match each heading in the online catalog to authority records. | A-N-U-F | |
| A-20 | set no limit on the number of authorities that can be linked to a bibliographic record. | A-N-U-F | |
| A-21 | allow manual maintenance of all fields of authority records online. | A-N-U-F | |
| A-22 | provide an alert if a field that is about to be edited is an authority-controlled field. | A-N-U-F | |
| A-23 | allow media centers/libraries in a union catalog to merge their authority records. | A-N-U-F | |
| A-24 | support global headings changes among authority files online. | A-N-U-F | |
| A-25 | save authority records. | A-N-U-F | |
| A-26 | print authority records alphabetically by: | | |
| | author. | A-N-U-F | |
| | series. | A-N-U-F | |
| | subject. | A-N-U-F | |
| | title. | A-N-U-F | |
| A-27 | print *see* and *see also* references. | A-N-U-F | |

| Feature Number | The system must: | Code: A-N-U-F | Scale: 1-5 |
|---|---|---|---|
| A-28 | disallow saving and exiting authority records without information input in the following fields, as applicable: | | |
| | geographical subject headings (tag 151). | A-N-U-F | |
| | fixed field (tag 008). | A-N-U-F | |
| | Leader. | A-N-U-F | |
| | main entry for corporate name (tag 110). | A-N-U-F | |
| | main entry for personal name (tag 100). | A-N-U-F | |
| | topical subject heading (tag 150). | A-N-U-F | |
| | other headings (please describe). | | |
| A-29 | generate and print partial and full reports, in alphabetical order, for: | A-N-U-F | |
| | name *see* headings. | A-N-U-F | |
| | name *see also* headings. | A-N-U-F | |
| | subject *see* headings. | A-N-U-F | |
| | subject *see also* headings. | A-N-U-F | |
| | series *see* headings. | A-N-U-F | |
| | series *see also* headings. | A-N-U-F | |
| A-30 | direct users from authorized headings to additional authorized headings for similar topics, and from unauthorized headings to authorized headings through cross-references. | A-N-U-F | |
| A-31 | allow authorities for withdrawn items to be purged if no other items are attached to the authorities. | A-N-U-F | |
| A-32 | allow insertion of tags, subfields, and diacritical marks. | A-N-U-F | |
| A-33 | Display see and see also references in the OPAC immediately after references are established. | A-N-U-F | |
| A-34 | Detect discrepancies between headings in bibliographic records and the headings in authority records. | A-N-U-F | |

**Figure 4.4 (Continued)**

| Feature Number | The system must: | Code: A-N-U-F | Scale: 1-5 |
|---|---|---|---|
| A-35 | Provide security through a password protection. | A-N-U-F | |

This space is provided for vendor comments and explanation.
Please use additional sheets if needed. Refer to features by the feature number (column 1).

## Figure 4.5. Essential specifications for the OPAC.

Codes for Column 3:   A = Available          Scale for Column 4   1-5:
                      N = Not available                      1 = Very poor
                      U = Under development                  5 = Excellent
                      F = Future development

**Note:** The term *must* means essential.

| Feature Number | The system must: | Code: A-N-U-F | Scale: 1-5 |
|---|---|---|---|
| O-1 | be Windows-based with a GUI interface. | | |
| O-2 | provide meaningful icons in the search and retrieval interfaces. | | |
| O-3 | allow navigation by using both a mouse and a computer keyboard keys. | | |
| O-4 | function concurrently with other modules in the system. | | |
| O-5 | function independently from other modules in the system. | | |
| O-6 | provides a Web-based OPAC compatible with the Z39.50 standard. | | |
| O-7 | allow searching by: | | |
| | a combination of search indexes (e.g., author/title, author/subject, etc.). | | |
| | author. | | |
| | barcode number. | | |
| | Boolean operators (AND, OR, NOT). | | |
| | call number. | | |
| | ISBN. | | |
| | ISSN. | | |
| | key phrase. | | |
| | keyword in author, title, subject, content notes, and series. | | |
| | LCCN. | | |
| | subjects. | | |
| | theme or material categories. | | |
| | title. | | |

**Figure 4.5 (Continued)**

| Feature Number | The system must: | Code: A-N-U-F | Scale: 1-5 |
|---|---|---|---|
| O-8 | provide hyperlink searching from:<br>   author fields<br>   subject fields<br>   series field<br>   other fields, please specify. | | |
| O-9 | display Web sites along with local records and label launch Web sites from a record with a point and click using a mouse. | | |
| O-10 | support use of commercial Web browsers (e.g., Netscape, Internet Explorer, etc.). | | |
| O-11 | support use of truncation and wild character in search statements to enhance information retrieval. | | |
| O-12 | maintain two modes of searching: simple and advanced. (Please provide examples of searches in both modes.) | | |
| O-13 | prohibit patrons from accessing other modules in the system from the OPAC. Security is provided through a password protection | | |
| O-14 | alert users about searches requiring a long time to process and suggest alternative methods of search refinement. | | |
| O-15 | allow nesting or provide automatic, intelligent nesting of search statements. (Please provide examples of nesting.) | | |
| O-16 | permit users to limit searches by:<br>   publication date.<br>   type of materials.<br>   intellectual and grade level.<br>   other levels (please specify). | | |
| O-17 | perform fast processing of searches with nesting, especially when more than three Boolean operators are used. | | |
| O-18 | provide an alphabetical list of keywords and allow browsing and selecting from the list. | | |

| Feature Number | The system must: | Code: A-N-U-F | Scale: 1-5 |
|---|---|---|---|
| O-19 | provide various display options of the results: | | |
| | card catalog format, with unlabeled fields | | |
| | card catalog format, with labeled fields | | |
| | MARC format, with unlabeled fields | | |
| | MARC format, with labeled fields | | |
| | other formats, please describe. | | |
| O-20 | support modification of search strategy. | | |
| O-21 | alert users about incorrect search parameters and provide means for remediation. | | |
| O-22 | ignore special diacritical marks and lower- and upper-case letters. | | |
| O-23 | forgive variations in punctuation and spacing. | | |
| O-24 | retrieve the "closest match" or provide a "sounds-like" feature in case of error in spelling or other type of error. | | |
| O-25 | disallow "no hits" and link a search statement to results in the union catalog in case of no hits in the local media center or library. | | |
| O-26 | retain users' search history on the screen. | | |
| O-27 | provide brief and full record display. | | |
| O-28 | allow users to terminate searches, especially long ones, easily and quickly. | | |
| O-29 | permit users to combine sets of search results. | | |
| O-30 | employ a list of stop words in search statements or alert users about removal of stop words from search statements. | | |
| O-31 | ignore stop words in search statements or alert users about removal of stop words from search statements. | | |
| O-32 | allow customization of screens (especially blocking certain features), displays, print functions, etc. | | |

**Figure 4.5 (Continued)**

| Feature Number | The system must: | Code: A-N-U-F | Scale: 1-5 |
|---|---|---|---|
| O-33 | provide an interface for searching by key-word with click-on boxes to indicate the Boolean operators to be used in a search. | | |
| O-34 | support adjacent or proximity searching. (Please describe the proximity operators used.) | | |
| O-35 | provide an online tutorial with meaningful examples of various kinds of searching. Context-sensitive online assistance must be available within all searches. | | |
| O-36 | return to a summary screen when a search yields more than one hit. | | |
| O-37 | allow browsing by complete call number (or part of one) and display a list of entries in call number order. | | |
| O-38 | permit users to select an entry by clicking on it with a mouse and by highlighting it and pressing the Enter/Return key, or by pressing the number of the desired entry. | | |
| O-39 | support setting the default display of an entry in a traditional card catalog format, a labeled card catalog format, or other format. | | |
| O-40 | allow searching by: | | |
| | full author name in direct and indirect order. | | |
| | full subject in direct and indirect order. | | |
| | full title. | | |
| | partial author name in direct and indirect order. | | |
| | partial subject in direct and indirect order. | | |
| | words in title. | | |
| O-41 | display the local titles, holdings, and locations from the media center or library where a search is conducted. | | |

| Feature Number | The system must: | Code: A-N-U-F | Scale: 1-5 |
|---|---|---|---|
| O-42 | display the titles, holdings, and locations of media centers or libraries in a union catalog at the option of the user.  A command or a function key for union catalog access must be present when results are displayed. | | |
| O-43 | display the status of an item retrieved based on the modules implemented. This includes but is not limited to: | | |
| | at the bindery. | | |
| | available. | | |
| | in circulation (with due date). | | |
| | in-processing. | | |
| | missing, lost, etc. | | |
| | on-order. | | |
| | on reserve. | | |
| | received. | | |
| | other (please specify). | | |
| O-44 | retain users' search history on the screen. | | |
| O-45 | provide brief and full record display. | | |
| O-46 | allow users to terminate searches, especially long ones, easily and quickly. | | |
| O-47 | permit users to combine sets of search results. | | |
| O-48 | employ a list of stop words in search statements or alert users about removal of stop words from search statements. | | |
| O-49 | ignore stop words in search statements or alert users about removal of stop words from search statements. | | |
| O-50 | match user search statements, in either direct or indirect format, with the standard correct format and retrieve information accordingly. | | |
| O-51 | sort search results in a variety of methods (e.g., alphabetically by author, title, subject, etc.). | | |

Figure 4.5 (Continued)

| Feature Number | The system must: | Code: A-N-U-F | Scale: 1-5 |
|---|---|---|---|
| O-52 | print search results to the screen | | |
| O-53 | allow cancellation of saved searches. | | |
| O-54 | provide automatic flip or display of *see* and *see also* references on the screen based on authority records. | | |
| O-55 | display search results in a MARC format at the option of the user. | | |
| O-56 | permit paging and scrolling easily within all searches. | | |
| O-57 | save search results to a floppy diskette and other media | | |
| O-58 | e-mail search results. | | |
| O-59 | support limiting the number of citations to be printed. | | |
| O-60 | display search results in alphabetical order. | | |
| O-61 | display the number of postings for each search statement on the screen. | | |
| O-62 | | | |
| O-63 | provide backup of the OPAC database as needed. | | |
| O-64 | restore the OPAC database as needed. | | |
| O-65 | allow specification of the fields to be key-word indexed. | | |
| O-66 | support the compilation and customization of bibliographies. Allow bibliography listings to be displayed on the screen for review before printing. | | |
| O-67 | provide search use statistics for: | | |
| | annual transactions for types of searches. (Please provide samples of search use statistics.) | | |
| | monthly transactions for types of searches. | | |
| | types of searches (e.g., author, title, subject, etc.) in novice and advanced search modes. | | |

| Feature Number | The system must: | Code: A-N-U-F | Scale: 1-5 |
|---|---|---|---|
| O-68 | allow turning search limiters on and off. | | |
| O-69 | disregard initial articles in the beginning of a search statement. | | |
| O-70 | return to the beginning of the search process when requested or after a reasonable timeout. (Please specify the timeout feature.) | | |
| O-71 | provide meaningful and easy-to-follow prompts throughout the search process. | | |
| O-72 | provide a *News* feature. | | |
| O-73 | be user-friendly and easy to use. | | |

**This space is provided for vendor comments and explanation.**
**Please use additional sheets if needed. Refer to features by the feature number (column 1).**

## Figure 4.6. Essential specifications for circulation.

| | |
|---|---|
| Codes for Column 3: | A = Available | Scale for Column 4   1-5: |
| | N = Not available | 1 = Very poor |
| | U = Under development | 5 = Excellent |
| | F = Future development | |

**Note:** The term *must* means essential.

| Feature Number | The system must: | Code: A-N-U-F | Scale: 1-5 |
|---|---|---|---|
| CR-1 | be Windows-based with a GUI interface. | | |
| CR-2 | allow navigation among different functions using a mouse and the computer keyboard. | | |
| CR-3 | allow definition of a minimum of three passwords to protect circulation functions: one for starting circulation, one for overriding block conditions, and one for changing circulation options. Please list other passwords that can be defined by staff. | | |
| CR-4 | allow the import of all U.S.MARC/MARC 21 records from the cataloging database and provides the option to display them in a brief MARC format. | | |
| CR-5 | support all circulation functions, including: | | |
| | Check-in. | | |
| | Check-out. | | |
| | Fines. | | |
| | Inventory. | | |
| | Overdues. | | |
| | Renewal. | | |
| | Housekeeping (e.g., resetting daily statistics reports). | | |
| | Reserve/hold. | | |
| | Management reports. | | |
| CR-6 | Function with other modules in the system. | | |
| CR-7 | function independently from other modules in the system. | | |

| Feature Number | The system must: | Code: A-N-U-F | Scale: 1-5 |
|---|---|---|---|
| CR-8 | display item status in the OPAC. | | |
| CR-9 | provide security through multiple password protection for all tasks. | | |
| CR-10 | provide an alert about records that are about to be deleted. | | |
| CR-11 | confirm deletion of records. | | |
| CR-12 | support partial and full inventory via a hand-held device. | | |
| CR-13 | accept manual keying and optical scanning of barcodes. | | |
| CR-14 | maintain a calendar and provide control for holidays and closing days. | | |
| CR-15 | support a minimum of 40 patron categories and 99 material types. | | |
| CR-16 | allow fines and due dates to vary with material codes and borrower types. | | |
| CR-17 | support renewal in a separate function. | | |
| CR-18 | allow customization of reports. | | |
| CR-19 | keep statistics for a minimum of two years. | | |
| CR-20 | support creation of borrower and item records on the fly. | | |
| CR-21 | support reserve/hold in a separate function. | | |
| CR-22 | allow the import of patron records into the patron database from external sources. Please list the student management software the system is compatible with. | | |
| CR-23 | support updating the database online. | | |
| CR-24 | allow customization of the database. | | |
| CR-25 | allow staff to define and override loan periods. | | |
| CR-26 | support global editing of patron records. | | |
| CR-27 | support global deletion of patron records. | | |
| CR-28 | provide a circulation log for various types of materials. | | |

**Figure 4.6 (Continued)**

| Feature Number | The system must: | Code: A-N-U-F | Scale: 1-5 |
|---|---|---|---|
| CR-29 | provide an audible or visual signal when a transaction is completed. | | |
| CR-30 | support context-sensitive help or a help index that is always present on all screens. | | |
| CR-31 | allow searching of patron records by: | | |
| | Barcode number. | | |
| | Patron ID number. | | |
| | Patron name (first or last). | | |
| | Other (please specify). | | |
| CR-32 | support initiation of a global due date in the entire database. | | |
| CR-33 | have a fast response time for all transactions. Please specify the response time for the following functions supported by an (**X**) microprocessor with a clock speed of (**X**) MHz: | | |
| | Composing overdues and fines for 50 items. | | |
| | Generating a report of overdues and fines for 50 items. | | |
| | Generating an inventory report for 50 scanned items. | | |
| | Generating a payment receipt. | | |
| | Scanning 50 barcode numbers at check-out and check-in. | | |
| | Scanning 50 barcode numbers using an inventory scanner. | | |
| CR-34 | support customization of a patron database by renaming the various fields. | | |
| CR-35 | accommodate a database of a minimum of (**X**) patron records and support its future growth to a minimum of (**X**) records. | | |
| CR-36 | support limiting the number of items circulated based on item category and patron type. | | |

| Feature Number | The system must: | Code: A-N-U-F | Scale: 1-5 |
|---|---|---|---|
| CR-37 | allow addition of fees to a patron record for damaged items, lost copies, etc. | | |
| CR-38 | calculate loan periods and due dates automatically according to: | | |
| | Closing days. | | |
| | Material type. | | |
| | Patron status or category. | | |
| | Other (please specify). | | |
| CR-39 | support variation in loan periods and due dates. | | |
| CR-40 | verify patron eligibility for item check-out. | | |
| CR-41 | maintain blocking features or traps. | | |
| CR-42 | alert staff about blocking features or traps at check-out. | | |
| CR-43 | accept and forgive partial and full fines. | | |
| CR-44 | allow due dates to be changed online. | | |
| CR-45 | display a patron history for items check out online, along with the titles check out, overdues, etc. | | |
| CR-46 | support a brief entry of a patron name, and provide a browsing list of names in alphabetical order. | | |
| CR-47 | provide an alert when a barcode is invalid, scanned, or keyed in incorrectly. | | |
| CR-48 | display the due dates and title of items on the terminal screen at the time of check-out. | | |
| CR-49 | maintain confidentiality of patron records, especially when item availability is displayed in OPAC. | | |
| CR-50 | support material check-out from any terminal. | | |
| CR-51 | allow multiple item check-out on a single ID. | | |

**Figure 4.6 (Continued)**

| Feature Number | The system must: | Code: A-N-U-F | Scale: 1-5 |
|---|---|---|---|
| CR-52 | place items back in circulation immediately after check-in. | | |
| CR-53 | provide an alert when a returned item does not belong to the local media center or library. | | |
| CR-54 | support item check-in or check-out using a barcode scanner. | | |
| CR-55 | support item check-in or check-out by keying in the barcode. | | |
| CR-56 | signal hold/reserve or other conditions at the time of check-in. | | |
| CR-57 | calculate overdues at the time of check-in and attach a fine to a patron record automatically. | | |
| CR-58 | support material check-in from any terminal. | | |
| CR-59 | give an audible or visual signal when a transaction is completed. | | |
| CR-60 | support fine control and print overdue notices in a variety of sequences. | | |
| CR-61 | provide a separate renewal function. | | |
| CR-62 | block renewal if an item is on hold. | | |
| CR-63 | block renewal if an item is overdue. | | |
| CR-64 | calculate and display new dates for renewals. | | |
| CR-65 | allow item renewal without scanning the item barcode (e.g., by phone). | | |
| CR-66 | produce a chronological queue for items on hold/reserve. | | |
| CR-67 | allow overriding a chronological queue for items on hold/reserve. | | |
| CR-68 | cancel a hold on an item automatically when the item is checked out, unless the item is on hold for other patrons in the queue.  In the latter case, it must readjust the hold queue. | | |
| CR-69 | cancel a hold on an item when the item is not claimed within a designated period of time. | | |

| Feature Number | The system must: | Code: A-N-U-F | Scale: 1-5 |
|---|---|---|---|
| CR-70 | cancel a hold on an item when an item is indicated lost or missing. | | |
| CR-71 | compose and print the following notices: | | |
| | Hold. | | |
| | Overdue. | | |
| | Recall. | | |
| | Renewal. | | |
| | Other (please specify). | | |
| CR-72 | create a patron record with the following information: | | |
| | Barcode number. | | |
| | Classification code. | | |
| | Full address. | | |
| | Full name. | | |
| | ID expiration date. | | |
| | ID or Social Security number. | | |
| | Location or homeroom number. | | |
| | Status or classification. | | |
| | Telephone number. | | |
| | Other (please specify). | | |
| CR-73 | support online editing or revision of information in a patron record. | | |
| CR-74 | print overdue reports for fines that are forgiven, partially paid, or paid in full. | | |
| CR-75 | sort overdue reports by: | | |
| | Call number of item. | | |
| | Patron address. | | |
| | Patron ID number. | | |
| | Patron location or homeroom number. | | |
| | Patron name. | | |
| | Title of item. | | |
| CR-76 | calculate fines for damaged or lost items. | | |
| CR-77 | support waiving fines. | | |

**Figure 4.6 (Continued)**

| Feature Number | The system must: | Code: A-N-U-F | Scale: 1-5 |
|---|---|---|---|
| CR-78 | print receipts for fines and fees paid. | | |
| CR-79 | include the following information for overdue notices: | | |
| | Author(s) of item(s). | | |
| | Call number of item(s). | | |
| | Date notice was prepared. | | |
| | Due date(s) of items. | | |
| | Patron address or homeroom number. | | |
| | Patron grade level. | | |
| | Patron ID number. | | |
| | Patron name. | | |
| | Title of item(s). | | |
| | Other (please specify). | | |
| CR-80 | allow customization of the format content of overdue lists or reports. | | |
| CR-81 | generate a list of lost or damaged items. | | |
| CR-82 | provide circulation statistics for a variety of circulation activities: | | |
| | Biweekly. | | |
| | Daily. | | |
| | Monthly. | | |
| | Weekly. | | |
| | Other frequency (please specify). | | |
| CR-83 | purge cleared transactions regularly, but retain the statistical data for management purposes. | | |
| CR-84 | save statistical reports. | | |

| Feature Number | The system must: | Code: A-N-U-F | Scale: 1-5 |
|---|---|---|---|
| CR-85 | provide circulation statistics and statistical reports for: | | |
| | Blocked patrons. | | |
| | Items lost and paid for. | | |
| | Items never circulated. | | |
| | Items on hold. | | |
| | List of deleted barcode numbers. | | |
| | List of patrons with expired cards. | | |
| | Lost items. | | |
| | Total fines paid to date. | | |
| | Total number of items check-out to date. | | |
| CR-86 | provide circulation statistics and statistical reports for a variety of circulation activities by: | | |
| | Call number. | | |
| | Grade level. | | |
| | Homeroom number or other location. | | |
| | Locally defined codes or categories. | | |
| | Patron status or category. | | |
| | Type of material. | | |
| CR-87 | list items previously reported lost but currently are on the shelves or in the circulation file. | | |
| CR-88 | print inventory reports for missing items, misshelved items, etc., in order by call number. | | |
| CR-89 | support partial and full inventory of materials. | | |
| CR-90 | print statistical reports based on locally defined formats. | | |
| CR-91 | provide detailed statistical reports for all circulation activities on: | | |
| | An annual basis. | | |
| | A daily basis. | | |
| | A monthly basis. | | |

**Figure 4.6 (Continued)**

| Feature Number | The system must: | Code: A-N-U-F | Scale: 1-5 |
|---|---|---|---|
| CR-92 | display statistical reports online before printing. | | |
| CR-93 | determine material use by: | | |
| | Dewey classification numbers. | | |
| | Patron status or category. | | |
| | Type of material. | | |
| | Other (please describe). | | |

**X =** to be filled in by the RFP preparer.

This space is provided for vendor comments and explanation.
Please use additional sheets if needed. Refer to features by the feature number (column 1).

## Figure 4.7. Essential specifications for acquisitions.

Codes for Column 3:  A = Available          Scale for Column 4   1-5:
                      N = Not available                   1 = Very poor
                      U = Under development               5 = Excellent
                  .   F = Future development

**Note:** The term *must* means essential.

| Feature Number | The system must: | Code: A-N-U-F | Scale: 1-5 |
|---|---|---|---|
| AC-1 | function concurrently with other modules in the system. | | |
| AC-2 | function independently of other modules in the system. | | |
| AC-3 | support various acquisitions functions, including: | | |
| | Material requests. | | |
| | Purchase orders. | | |
| | Receiving. | | |
| | Claiming. | | |
| | Cancellation. | | |
| | Verification of items against outstanding orders. | | |
| | Verification of items against existing materials in OPAC. | | |
| | Budget and fund accounting. | | |
| AC-4 | interface online with material suppliers to support ordering, inquiries, claiming, and other related tasks. | | |

**Figure 4.7 (Continued)**

| Feature Number | The system must: | Code: A-N-U-F | Scale: 1-5 |
|---|---|---|---|
| AC-5 | allow searching of records by: | | |
| | Author. | | |
| | Title. | | |
| | Publication date. | | |
| | ISBN. | | |
| | LCCN. | | |
| | Publisher name. | | |
| | Purchase order number. | | |
| | Order date. | | |
| | Requester's name. | | |
| | Vendor's or supplier's name. | | |
| | Fund code. | | |
| AC-6 | prepare and print: | | |
| | Purchase orders. | | |
| | Invoices. | | |
| | Payment vouchers. | | |
| AC-7 | allow: | | |
| | Customization of purchase orders. | | |
| | Encumbrance of funds. | | |
| | Adjustment of funds as material receipt is input. | | |
| | Creation of new accounts. | | |
| AC-8 | provide an alert about insufficient funds for ordering. | | |
| AC-9 | support overcommitments of funds. | | |
| AC-10 | support multiple fund codes for media centers or libraries in a union catalog. | | |
| AC-11 | allow multiple copies to be ordered for multiple media centers or libraries in the union catalog. | | |
| AC-12 | allow deletion of vendor records online. | | |
| AC-13 | support one order for multiple copies. | | |

| Feature Number | The system must: | Code: A-N-U-F | Scale: 1-5 |
|---|---|---|---|
| AC-14 | automatically display acquisitions status in OPAC as item status is modified. | | |
| AC-15 | support reviewing all orders online before printing or sending them electronically. | | |
| AC-16 | generate a list of materials not received within a set time period. | | |
| AC-17 | track materials not received within a set time period. | | |
| AC-18 | maintain a file to include information about each vendor and facilitate material acquisition.  Vendor file must include: | | |
| | Account number. | | |
| | Address. | | |
| | Name. | | |
| | Fax number. | | |
| | Telephone number. | | |
| AC-19 | store full and partial acquisitions records with the following information: | | |
| | Author. | | |
| | Cost. | | |
| | Fund code. | | |
| | ISBN. | | |
| | Number of copies requested. | | |
| | Publication date. | | |
| | Title. | | |
| | Type of binding. | | |
| | Vendor name. | | |
| | Other (please specify). | | |
| AC-20 | permit setting and changing the timing for cancellation. | | |
| AC-21 | issue claims for materials not received within a set time period, change the status from "on order" to "claimed," and provide the date of the claim. | | |

**Figure 4.7 (Continued)**

| Feature Number | The system must: | Code: A-N-U-F | Scale: 1-5 |
|---|---|---|---|
| AC-22 | support cancellation of orders and allow transfer of canceled orders to another vendor file to issue new orders. | | |
| AC-23 | print cancellation notices, lists, or letters to both vendors and requesters. | | |
| AC-24 | change item status from "on order " to "canceled" and provide the date of cancellation. | | |
| AC-25 | change item status from "on order" to "received" and provide the date of receipt. | | |
| AC-26 | track vendor performance and provide performance statistics. | | |
| AC-27 | prepare budget reports with funds encumbered, spent, and available. | | |
| AC-28 | set back funds to zero at the end of the fiscal year. | | |
| AC-29 | keep statistics for a minimum of two years. | | |
| AC-30 | provide password protection. | | |
| AC-31 | support database backup and restoration. | | |
| AC-32 | prepare and generate statistical reports for the following: | | |
| | Canceled items. | | |
| | Claimed items. | | |
| | Items not yet received. | | |
| | Items on order. | | |
| | Received items. | | |
| | Returned items. | | |
| | Unavailable items (e.g., out-of-print). | | |
| | Other. (Please describe and provide samples of reports.) | | |

**This space is provided for vendor comments and explanation.**
**Please use additional sheets if needed. Refer to features by the feature number (column 1).**

## Figure 4.8. Essential specifications for serials.

Codes for Column 3: A = Available      Scale for Column 4   1-5:
           N = Not available                1 = Very poor
           U = Under development        5 = Excellent
           F = Future development

**Note:** The term *must* means essential.

| Feature Number | The system must: | Code: A-N-U-F | Scale: 1-5 |
|---|---|---|---|
| S-1 | function concurrently with other modules in the system. | | |
| S-2 | function independently of other modules in the system. | | |
| S-3 | support various serials functions, including: | | |
| | Bindery management. | | |
| | Budget and fund accounting. | | |
| | Cancellation. | | |
| | Check-in. | | |
| | Claiming. | | |
| | Ordering. | | |
| | Renewal. | | |
| | Routing. | | |
| S-4 | manager and maintain serials holdings. | | |
| S-5 | accommodate all types of serials, including but not limited to: | | |
| | Annuals or yearbooks. | | |
| | Journals and magazines. | | |
| | Newspapers. | | |
| | Periodical indexes. | | |
| S-6 | accommodate various frequencies as well as special and irregular issues. | | |
| S-7 | adjust changes in frequencies, titles, publishers, etc. | | |
| S-8 | produce routing slips. | | |
| S-9 | interface online with serials vendors to support electronic ordering, inquiries, claiming, and other related tasks. | | |

**Figure 4.8 (Continued)**

| Feature Number | The system must: | Code: A-N-U-F | Scale: 1-5 |
|---|---|---|---|
| S-10 | support reviewing all orders online before printing or sending them electronically. | | |
| S-11 | allow searching by: | | |
| | Boolean operators. | | |
| | CODEN. | | |
| | Date of first issue. | | |
| | ISSN. | | |
| | Keyword. | | |
| | Other dates. | | |
| | Publisher. | | |
| | Title. | | |
| | Vendor. | | |
| | Other (please specify). | | |
| S-12 | store full and partial serials records with the following information: | | |
| | Fund code. | | |
| | ISSN. | | |
| | Subscription cost. | | |
| | Title. | | |
| | Vendor name. | | |
| | Volume, issue, and date. | | |
| | Other (please specify). | | |
| S-13 | support one order for multiple copies. | | |
| S-14 | support multiple fund codes for media centers or libraries in a union catalog. | | |
| S-15 | maintain a vendor file to include, but not limited to: | | |
| | Account number. | | |
| | Address. | | |
| | Fax number. | | |
| | Name. | | |
| | Telephone number. | | |

| Feature Number | The system must: | Code: A-N-U-F | Scale: 1-5 |
|---|---|---|---|
| S-16 | support: Encumbrance of funds. | | |
| | Adjustment of funds as serials are received. | | |
| | Creation of new accounts. | | |
| S-17 | allow multiple copies to be ordered for multiple members in the union catalog. | | |
| S-18 | provide an alert about insufficient funds for ordering. | | |
| S-19 | track volumes or issues not received within a set time period and generate claims automatically. | | |
| S-20 | prepare budget reports with funds encumbered, spent, and available. | | |
| S-21 | set back funds to zero at the end of the fiscal year. | | |
| S-22 | change the status of claimed serials from "on order" to "claimed," and provide the date of the claim. | | |
| S-23 | automatically display item status in OPAC as status is modified. | | |
| S-24 | support setting and changing the timing for cancellation. | | |
| S-25 | change item status from "on order" to "canceled," and provide the date of cancellation. | | |
| S-26 | allow the input of messages about changes in serials titles, publishers, etc. | | |

**Figure 4.8 (Continued)**

| Feature Number | The system must: | Code: A-N-U-F | Scale: 1-5 |
|---|---|---|---|
| S-27 | prepare and generate statistical reports for the following: | | |
| | Received items. | | |
| | Canceled items. | | |
| | Renewed items. | | |
| | Claimed items. | | |
| | Routed items. | | |
| | Items not yet received. | | |
| | Items on order. | | |
| | Other. (Please describe and provide samples of reports.) | | |
| S-28 | keep statistics for a minimum of two years. | | |
| S-29 | track vendor performance and provide performance statistics. | | |
| S-30 | allow deletion of vendor records online. | | |

This space is provided for vendor comments and explanation.
Please use additional sheets if needed. Refer to features by the feature number (column 1).

# Chapter 5

---

## Preparing the Collection
## for the Automated System

---

Implementation is the most time-consuming activity in any automation project. It entails a wide range of activities, including collection preparation, database creation through retrospective conversion (recon), barcoding, site preparation, software installation, user training, and database evaluation and maintenance. Because implementation is such an extensive topic, it has been divided into two chapters for the purposes of this discussion. This chapter describes the various stages and activities related to the collection itself. Chapter 6 deals with the issues related to facilities, installation, and ongoing use and management of the automated system. Although the discussion of these topics has been divided for purposes of this book, it is important to remember that an integrated automation system requires integrated implementation; the steps taken in preparing the collection will affect later stages of implementation, and how the system will be used and managed must be taken into account during the collection preparation.

Implementation activities related to the collection itself are collection preparation, retrospective conversion (recon), and barcoding. Retrospective conversion is a key step in implementing an automated system. Simply put, recon involves converting the information from the card catalog format into a computer-readable format using acceptable bibliographic standards (i.e., MARC 21). The shelflist is used to obtain the information from the card catalog. A shelflist is part of the card catalog that contains one master card for each item owned by the library; master cards are arranged by a classification number, such as a Dewey Decimal Classification number.

# COLLECTION PREPARATION

Collection preparation is an essential prerequisite for recon. Adequate collection preparation—weeding, inventorying the collection, and analyzing the shelflist—saves both time and money in recon.

## Weeding

Every media center or library should have a weeding policy or a set of criteria to use in judging which materials are to be withdrawn, replaced, or repaired, as well as what to do with materials that are withdrawn from the collection. The policy or criteria should guide the media center or library staff in weeding the entire collection as a first step in preparing the collection for recon.

After weeding is completed, shelflist cards for withdrawn items must be removed. Withdrawn materials may be discarded, exchanged with other media centers or libraries, or otherwise disposed of based on material disposition guidelines or policy.

Every media center or library has weeding criteria outlined in its collection development policy. The main criteria for weeding are appearance and condition, poor content, age (except for classics, archives, and materials of historical value), inappropriateness to age level or clientele, and duplicates that are no longer needed.

In doing the recon, automation vendors review the shelflist, matching each item in the shelflist against the MARC database. Usually, vendors charge for each item matched against the shelflist. By weeding, one reduces the number of items to be converted into a MARC format and, therefore, curtails the cost of recon. Weeding produces savings in time and money even when recon is performed in-house; weeding the collection before beginning recon prevents staff from converting items that are not needed in the collection.

## Inventory

A thorough inventory is essential to identify items for which no shelflist cards exist and to identify shelflist cards for which materials are missing or lost. A decision should be made with regard to the kinds of materials to be converted. All materials that are destined for conversion must have shelflist cards. Sometimes, automation vendors allow title page copying and sending of items that do not have shelflist cards. When title pages are used, make sure you transcribe the same information needed for recon (e.g., ISBN, LCCN holdings, etc.).

## Shelflist Analysis

Shelflist analysis is performed to examine the completeness and accuracy of the shelflist, including variations in and consistency of items' call numbers, locations, and prefixes. All materials to be converted should have shelflist cards, and those cards should be as complete and accurate as possible. The more complete and accurate the cards are, the higher the probability is for finding matches in MARC databases. Recon is performed by matching shelflist cards against MARC databases, then copying the appropriate MARC records onto a disk or other medium. MARC records can also be transferred electronically from the Web to a media center or a library's computer workstation. (More detail about this process is provided later in this chapter.) These records, put together, form the database on which the automated system is based. The quality of recon, whether in-house or off-site (i.e., outsourced to a vendor), begins with the accuracy and completeness of the shelflist. Therefore, adequate time should be devoted to cleaning up and standardizing the shelflist.

The benefits of a standardized shelflist go beyond recon. Uniformity and consistency will serve patrons better by making information retrieval more effective, especially in a union catalog environment.

In analyzing the shelflist, make sure that each card contains the following information:

> Accurate bibliographic information (e.g., author, title, publication information);
>
> A call number and a standard prefix (e.g., B921 for individual biographies, R or REF for reference);
>
> Number of copies held, so that a barcode can be generated for each copy;
>
> Number of volumes held (for multivolume items), so that a barcode can be generated for each volume;
>
> Complete bibliographic information, including subject headings, ISBN, LCCN, and ISSN, for each item, as applicable.

Usually, the vendor you hire to do the recon sends you guidelines for packing the shelflist. The vendor may also send you a call number verification form. Follett Software Company's call number verification form, for example, contains information about main entry, call number prefixes and suffixes, and upper- versus lowercase letters to use for call numbers. The form has the following eight categories, with options in each: fiction, nonfiction, individual biography, collective biography, easy books, reference, story collection, and professional collection (Follett Software Company 2000). The media specialist or information professional will place a checkmark next to the option it chooses for its collection. Such forms save time in standardizing the shelflist. If the vendor does not have such a form, develop one yourself and send it with your shelflist.

# RETROSPECTIVE CONVERSION

Retrospective conversion involves converting a shelflist into a machine-readable format based on recognized bibliographic standards (i.e., MARC 21) for the purpose of creating a database that supports the operation of an automated system. This is generally done by searching for each and every item in the shelflist in one or more standard bibliographic databases. Whenever a match is found—that is, whenever a MARC record in the bibliographic database exactly matches the item in the shelflist—the record from the database is saved onto a diskette or other medium. These saved records will form the bibliographic database that supports the automated system.

## Specifications for Recon

Developing specifications for recon allows you to customize the content of the automated system's MARC database and thus maintain consistency in its format. Specifications stipulate what to include and exclude from each MARC record and also identify which fields require editing, enhancement, or special attention. Regardless of the method of conversion used (vendor, in-house, or a combination), specifications for recon should be established.

This will clarify for the vendor or in-house staff what is expected of them and will ensure that the finished product meets the needs and requirements of the media center or library. It also gives the vendor a profile of the MARC records to use not only in performing recon but also in filling future orders for MARC records (e.g., a media center or library might periodically order MARC records for newly purchased materials). Specifications may stipulate the following:

- *Special MARC fields and enhancements*: the MARC fields to include. Specifications in these fields may include, for example, that "all MARC records must contain the tag 505 for contents note, the tag 520 for summary note, the tag 521 for grade level, and the tag 856 for URL addresses." See Furrie (2000) for various MARC 21 tags.

- *Classification numbers*: the number to include, exclude, verify, or edit. A specification in this area may include, for example, that "Dewey numbers should be edited for their length and that long numbers that are supplied by the Library of Congress should be truncated at the first prime mark." A prime mark is a symbol that identifies the location where a Dewey number should be truncated. Example: 025'.00285. Media centers or libraries that have a few titles about library automation (025) may choose to truncate this Dewey number at the prime mark (i.e., 025) instead of including the whole number.

- *Subject headings*: the headings to include, exclude, verify, or edit (e.g., *Sears List of Subject Headings*, *Library of Congress Subject Headings List*, *Library of Congress Children's List*). A specification in this area may indicate, for example, that "all subject headings must contain headings from *Sears List of Subject Headings*."

- *Record format*: the provision of full MARC 21 records based on *AACR2R* and ISBD standards. A specification in this area may state, for example, that "all records must comply with the MARC 21 standard."

- *MARC designators*: the inclusion of the components of a full MARC record. Specifications in this area may stipulate, for example, that "a full MARC record must contain the Leader (tag 000), fixed field (tag 008), variable control fields (tags 001-009), and variable data fields (tags 010-900)."

- *Other areas*: the provision of specific elements, such as General Material Description (GMD) for all nonprint materials and prefixes for call numbers (e.g., R for reference, B for biographies, V for videotapes). A specification in this area may state, for example, that "GMD must be included for all nonprint materials."

- *Recon databases*: the extraction of MARC records from the Library of Congress (LC) database, contributors' databases, the Library of Canada database, and other databases. A specification in this area may state, for example, that "only LC records are accepted" and that "non-matched items should be flagged and keyed-in in full MARC 21 format at no or marginal additional cost."

- *Accuracy rate:* The matched records should be as accurate as possible. A specification in this case might state, for example, that "the accuracy rate of matched records must not fall below 98 percent."

Developing specifications for recon requires adequate knowledge of the various components of a MARC record format. Knowledge of *AACR2R* is a prerequisite for understanding MARC records and for maintaining consistency in the content of the MARC database.

# Who Does It?

A database can be created off-site by an automation vendor, in-house by a media specialist or information professional or trained staff, or by a combination of the two methods. Each option has advantages and disadvantages. Selecting an option depends on the cost, the knowledge and skill of the staff who will carry out the conversion in-house, staffing, and the timeline for implementing the automation project.

# Vendor Conversion Process

This process requires that a shelflist be prepared, packed, and shipped based on the guidelines provided by the recon vendor. (It is highly recommended that the shelflist be insured so that it can be tracked in case it is lost in shipping. If you send it "return receipt requested," you will know when it arrives at the vendor's site.) After receiving the shelflist, the vendor assigns one or more operators to perform the conversion.

The procedure for converting the shelflist is fairly straightforward. An operator searches one or more master MARC 21 databases to find a match for each shelflist card. Searches are done by LCCN, ISBN, or another standard parameter. Matched MARC records are saved to diskettes or other media (to be sent to the media center or library). Records can also be transferred electronically (using file transfer protocol, FTP) to a media center's or library's computer workstation. Some vendors edit and enhance the records for an additional fee. The vendor then links a barcode to each record; because this barcode identifies the linked record, it is called a *smart* barcode. Upon completion of recon, the vendor returns the shelflist to the media center or library, along with the diskettes containing the MARC records (if this was the agreed-upon option) and smart barcode labels.

Inevitably, some shelflist cards will not be matched in the MARC databases used; these records are either created manually by the vendor (operator) or can be returned to the media center or library. Records for the returned cards can be created in-house after the cataloging database has been implemented, or they can be matched against a database of MARC records at a neighboring library or at the district library. Other options are to lease a MARC database on CD-ROM or use a Web-based MARC database. (See "In-House Conversion Process" for more information about this process.)

## *Advantages*

The vendor conversion process has the following advantages:

- It allows the media specialist or information professional to engage in other activities on site.

- It provides faster completion of database creation; first, because the operators are well versed in the procedure, and second, because the vendor may assign several full-time operators to work on the project. This is not likely to happen if recon is done in-house.

- The turnaround time for completion of the recon can be predicted. This helps planners and managers establish a schedule for implementing the automated system.

- It may generate a high match rate, especially when more than one database is used.

- Records for unmatched items may be created by the operator, thus saving library staff and time.

- Smart barcodes (i.e., barcodes containing the name of the media center or library, title of the item, call number, and other information, as specified) are linked to their respective items during recon and are supplied with converted items.

- Authority records may be linked to converted items, thus saving time for creating cross-references after implementing the automated system.

## *Disadvantages*

The vendor conversion process has the following disadvantages:

- The conversion may not be completed on time as scheduled.

- The shelflist may be lost in transit.

- There is always a possibility of mismatches and errors. Database cleanup is highly recommended. This is performed after the MARC records (supplied by the vendor on diskettes or other media) are downloaded into the cataloging database.

- The absence of the shelflist from the media center or library may make it difficult to answer some users' questions. For example, if a user needs information about an item, and that information is not provided on the item's catalog card but is provided on the shelflist card, then, in the absence of the shelflist, that user's question cannot be answered. A user may wish to know, for example, how many volumes of a particular work the library owns; this information may appear on the shelflist but not on catalog cards.

## *Choosing a Vendor*

Many companies offer recon service. Auto-Graphics, Inc., Follett Software Company, Sagebrush Corporation, Brodart Automation, and MARCIVE, Inc., are just a few. In selecting a specific vendor for recon, consider the following:

- The MARC database used to extract the records. The Library of Congress database is preferred because it is authoritative.

- The size of the MARC databases consulted and the type of records included (e.g., print, nonprint). For a small collection, a vendor's MARC database should contain more than 2 million records. For a larger collection, a vendor's database should contain more than 4 million records. (You may wish to include this as a criterion in selecting a recon vendor.)

- The qualifications of the operators responsible for the recon. The more skilled the operators are at applying bibliographic standards (i.e., MARC 21, *AACR2R*, etc.), the higher the accuracy rate will be. The accuracy rate should not fall below 98 percent.

- The vendor's experience in providing recon service. (At least five years' experience is recommended.)

- The kind of enhancements that the vendor is willing to apply to various fields in MARC records, as well as the cost of those enhancements.

- The quality of MARC records. Records must be as complete as possible. Media specialists or information professionals should compare samples of MARC records from various vendors before making a final decision on which vendor to use.

- The search parameters used to find matches from shelflist cards (e.g., author, subject, series, title), their compatibility with the Library of Congress, and the cost.

- The cost of converting each matched item, providing a full MARC record.

- The cost of keying-in or creating a full (or brief) MARC record for items that had no matches.

- The turnaround time for completing the conversion.

- The vendor's reputation and reliability.

- The clarity of the vendor's guidelines for packing and shipping the shelflist.

It is highly recommended that you obtain sample MARC records from the recon vendors under consideration. Examine and compare the quality of these records. You may also want to examine MARC records that have been created or matched by these vendors for media centers or libraries that are located in your district or a nearby area. The comparison of MARC records will help you make a good decision about the vendor to choose for recon.

## In-House Conversion Process

The in-house recon task consists of matching each shelflist card against one or more MARC database(s). Searches for MARC record matches are performed using LCCN, ISBN, and/or other parameters. Records found are edited and enhanced, as needed, and a barcode is linked to each matched record. Records are then saved onto computer diskettes or other media. These saved MARC records should be stored in a safe, secure place. These records will be downloaded into the cataloging module after it is implemented.

### Options

There are four main options for doing the in-house conversion: Use one or more CD-ROM MARC database(s), subscribe to fee-based Web services, use Web services that provide free MARC records, and create MARC records manually.

### CD-ROM

Many automation software companies offer MARC records on CD-ROM databases on a subscription basis. The most popular MARC databases available are *Bibliofile* (The Library Corporation), *Precision One* (Brodart Automation), *Alliance Plus* (Follett Software Company), and *LaserQuest* (GRCI Library Systems). A current description of each of these databases is found on each respective company's Web site. (See Table 5.1.)

## Table 5.1. Selected Recon Vendors

| Vendor Name and Address* | Vendor Name and Address |
|---|---|
| **Auto-graphics, Inc.**<br>3201 Temple Ave.<br>Pomona, CA 91768-3200<br>Phone: (800) 776-6939<br>E-mail: info@auto-graphics.com<br>URL: http://www.auto-graphics.com | **Library Associates (FastCat)**<br>8845 W. Olympic Blvd., Suite 201A<br>Beverly Hills, CA 90211<br>Phone: (800) 987-6794<br>E-mail: fastcat@primenet.com<br>URL: http://www.libraryassociates.com |
| **Brodart Automation**<br>500 Arch St.<br>Williamsport, PA 17705<br>Phone: (800) 233-8467, ext. 640<br>E-mail: salesmkt@brodart.com<br>URL: http://www.brodart.com | **The Library Corporation (TLC)**<br>Research Park<br>Inwood, WV 25428<br>Phone: (800) 325-7759<br>URL: http://www.tlcdelivers.com |
| **ComPanion Corporation**<br>1831 Fort Union Blvd.<br>Salt Lake City, UT 84121<br>Phone: (800) 347-6439<br>URL: http://companionCorp.com | **The Library of Congress**<br>Cataloging Service Division<br>Washington, D.C. 20541-4912<br>Phone: (202) 707-6100<br>E-mail: cdsinfo@loc.gov<br>URL: http://lcweb.loc.gov/cds/mds.html |
| **Follett Software Company**<br>1391 Corporate Dr.<br>McHenry, IL 60050<br>Phone: (800) 323-3397<br>E-mail:<br>URL: http://www.fsc.follett.com | **MARCIVE, Inc.**<br>P.O.Box 47508<br>San Antonio, TX 78265-7508<br>Phone: (800) 531-7678<br>E-mail: info@marcive.com<br>URL: http://www.marcive.com |
| **Gaylord Information Systems**<br>P.O.Box 4901<br>Syracuse, NY 13221-4901<br>Phone: (800) 272-3414<br>E-mail: willis@gaylord.com<br>URL: http://www.gaylord.com | **Sagebrush Corporation**<br>457 East South St.<br>Caledonia, MN 55921<br>Phone: (800) 654-3002<br>E-mail: info@sagebrushcorp.com<br>URL: http://www.sagebrushcorp.com |

| Vendor Name and Address* | Vendor Name and Address |
|---|---|
| **A-G Canada, Ltd.**<br>3300 Bloor St. West<br>9th Floor, Center Tower<br>Toronto, Ontario M8X 2X3<br>Phone: (800) 225-8534, ext. 307<br>E-mail: bam@ag-canada.com<br>URL: http://www.ag-canada.com | **SIRS Mandarin, Inc.**<br>P.O. Box 272348<br>Boca Raton, FL<br>33427-2348<br>Phone: (800) 232-7477<br>E-mail: custserve@sirs.com<br>URL: http://www.sirs.com |
| **LaserQuest**<br>GRCI Library Systems<br>5383 Hollister Ave.<br>Santa Barbara, Ca 93111<br>Phone (800) 933-5383<br>E-mail: dcook@grci.com<br>URL: http://www.grci.com | **SLC (Special Libraries Cataloging) Services**<br>4493 Lindholm Rd.<br>Victoria, BC V9C 3Y1 Canada<br>Phone: (250) 474-3361<br>E-mail: mac@slc.bc.ca<br>URL: http://www.slc.bc.ca |

* All URLs were last accessed on October 29, 2001.

## Fee-Based Web Services

A few software companies that provide their MARC databases on CD-ROM have also made them accessible via the Web for a fee. One of these databases is ITS.MARC (the equivalent database to *Bibliofile* on CD-ROM), provided by The Library Corporation (TLC). ITS.MARC (http://www.itsmarc.com) has the largest database of MARC records (over 5 million) and offers records in the English language and foreign languages. The database is easy to use. MARC records can be edited and enhanced online before they are downloaded onto one's computer diskette or hard drive. Downloaded records can be imported into one's local automated system. A thirty-day trial is available through the company's Web site. Another popular fee-based Web database to use for recon is EZCat/Pro from Book Systems (http://www.booksys.com/ezcatpro/maininfo.html). Like ITS.MARC, this database is easy to search, and MARC records can be edited and enhanced online before they are imported into a local automated system. EZCat/Pro is available for one-time software purchase instead of a subscription fee, which makes it more economical for small media centers or libraries. An online demo of this software package can be downloaded from the Company's Web site for free. EZCat/Pro may work best with the company's Concourse automation software, although Book Systems claims that EZCat/Pro is compatible with any automation software package that imports U.S.MARC.

## Web-Based Free MARC Records

The availability of Web-based union catalogs in the public domain has facilitated access to MARC records and made cataloging less time-consuming for many media specialists and information professionals, especially those who work in media centers or libraries with limited budgets and, hence, cannot afford fee-based services. As of the writing of this book, there is one main Web service that performs a similar function to EZCat/Pro, except that it is free of charge. LibraryCom (http://www.librarycom.com/\lc.exe/Freemarc), also known as MARC for Schools, is provided by CASPR Library Systems, a well-known automation company. This database is easy to search. It is a Web database for K–12 schools. MARC records can be saved and downloaded onto a computer diskette or hard drive and then imported into a local automated system. It has a CD-ROM equivalent that is available for a fee.

An additional option for finding MARC records on the Web free of charge is to search Web-based union catalogs, such as SUNLINK (http://www.sunlink.ucf.edu), a database of Florida K–12 libraries, and TLC (http://www.auto-graphics.com/cgiojw/redir?txlc), a database of Texas K–12 libraries. Note that before you import MARC records into your database from any Web sites, consult with the sales consultant of your automated system to ensure that such a task will not corrupt your database. Remember that not all MARC records that you find in union catalogs are accurate and of a high quality. You may need to edit these records after or before you import them into your database. Although use of free MARC services facilitates cataloging, not to mention saving time and money, I do not recommend that you rely on this type of service solely for doing your recon, mainly because Web sites are volatile; that is, they may disappear without notice. In addition, many MARC records available from these and other Web sites contain errors in cataloging.

You may create MARC records manually by cataloging items using the automated system's cataloging module after the automated system has been installed. Every item in the collection that is destined for recon will be input into the system. Performing this task requires adequate knowledge of cataloging rules (*AACR2R*) and the MARC 21 standard. Some automated systems (Winnebago Spectrum, Follett Cir/Cat) offer an "easy" MARC entry that allows input of bibliographic information in a non-MARC format. Once an item's information has been saved, the automated system transforms it into a MARC format. Creating MARC records in this manner for the entire collection can be a daunting and time-consuming task and may result in a high level of inaccuracy. However, this option is the only way to catalog items for which MARC records are not found in any vendor's database or on the Web.

## Advantages

In-house conversion has the following advantages:

- The shelflist remains in the media center or library.

- The media specialist's or information professional's firsthand knowledge of the collection and the shelflist may generate a higher accuracy rate than vendor recon will.

- Using the Web to find MARC record matches can be done from home or any other location where an Internet connection is available. This process can expedite record conversion and may result in a higher recon accuracy rate, because the person who is doing the conversion is not interrupted frequently to serve patrons. In addition, use of more than one Web-based recon service will generate a higher number of record matches.

## *Disadvantages*

The disadvantages of in-house conversion outnumber the advantages. Some of the disadvantages follow:

- CD-ROM databases may contain fewer MARC records than databases used by a vendor, resulting in a lower match rate. If a media center or library cannot afford subscribing to more than one CD-ROM database, staff can find record matches via Web services that make their MARC databases available at no cost. As mentioned previously, there is no guarantee of the availability of these services in the future. Media specialists or information professionals may have to compromise on the quality of MARC records they find in databases in the public domain.

- Most CD-ROM databases are updated only monthly or quarterly. This causes a backlog of unmatched items.

- The conversion may take a long time to complete, especially if the media center or library is understaffed. The larger the collection, the longer it will take to complete the conversion.

- Media center or library services, such as user assistance, may be diminished because of staff time devoted to the conversion.

- Constant interruption of staff may result in a high error rate, which in return will affect the quality of the database.

- The larger the collection, the greater the cost of labor will be. (See the cost analysis below for a comparison of the costs of vendor and in-house recon.)

- Any hardware or software failure will delay the conversion. In addition, Web-based services may be extremely slow when Internet traffic is high.

# Combined Conversion Process

This process involves having part of the collection converted by a vendor and part of it converted by media center or library staff. For example, nonprint materials may be converted in-house, and print materials may be outsourced to a vendor. The same procedures for recon mentioned previously are followed. The advantages and disadvantages of this conversion process combine those of both the vendor and in-house conversions.

# Cost Analysis for Vendor versus In-House Recon

Before deciding on a conversion method, perform a cost analysis to determine the most cost-effective and efficient method of conversion. Cost analysis provides justification for choosing a specific method of conversion. A sample cost analysis comparing vendor and in-house conversion is provided here as a guideline. Adapt it to your own situation to estimate and compare the cost of each conversion method.

## *Cost Analysis for Vendor Conversion*

Estimating the cost of vendor conversion should be based on

> The number of items to be converted,
>
> The enhancements that must be made to the records,
>
> The cost of the smart barcodes,
>
> The cost of spine labels, and
>
> The cost of insurance and shipping.

Assume that you have a collection of 5,000 items and that the vendor charges $.50 per item converted and $.05 for each enhancement based on your specifications. The lowest estimated cost would be:

| | | |
|---|---|---|
| 5,000 items @ $.50 per item | = | $2,500 |
| 5,000 items @ $.05 per enhancement | = | $250 |
| 5,000 items @ $.05 per smart barcode linked | = | $250 |
| 5,000 labels @ $.05 per label | = | $250 |
| Insurance | = | $50 |
| Shipping | = | $50 |
| Total | = | **$3,350** |

## *Cost Analysis for In-House Conversion*

Assume that you are considering in-house conversion using a CD-ROM database of MARC records. Your lowest cost estimate should be based on

> The cost of subscribing to a CD-ROM database for one year (or a fee-based Web service) and
>
> The cost of subscribing to an additional CD-ROM database for nonprint materials or other materials, barcode labels, and labor.

Recon can be performed by a professional or paraprofessional. Because the cost of labor is involved, the cost of the conversion varies by salary. Using a collection size of 5,000 items, the total cost of conversion performed by a professional will range from $8,305 to $17,044, whereas the cost will be about $7,881when completed by a paraprofessional.

### Highest Cost Estimate for Conversion by a Professional

Assume that the collection of 5,000 items is going to be converted by a professional on staff. The highest cost estimate would be:

| | | |
|---|---|---|
| Salary for ten months | = | $29,000 |
| Hourly rate = $2,900 per month/160 hours per month (40 hours per week) | = | $18 per hour |
| Average number of minutes to convert, edit, enhance an item, and generate a barcode | = | 10 minutes |
| Number of minutes needed = 5,000 x 10 | = | 50,000 minutes |
| Number of hours needed = 50,000/60 | = | 833 hours |
| Labor cost = 833 x $18 | = | **$14,994** |

| Subscription to a CD-ROM database | = | $ | 900 per year |
|---|---|---|---|
| Subscription to a CD-ROM database for nonprint materials | = | $ | 900 per year |
| Smart barcode production software | = | $ | 250 |
| Total | = | | $17,044 |

## Lowest Cost Estimate for Conversion by a Professional

Suppose that the conversion time per item is reduced from ten to five minutes because of experience. Then, the lowest cost estimate will be:

| Salary for ten months | = | $24,000 |
|---|---|---|
| Hourly rate = $2,900 per month/160 hours per month (40 hours per week) | = | $15 per hour |
| Average number of minutes to convert, edit, enhance an item, and generate a barcode | = | 5 minutes |
| Number of minutes needed = 5,000 x 5 | = | 25,000 minutes |
| Number of hours needed = 25,000/60 | = | 418 hours |
| Labor cost = 417 x $15 | = | $ 6,255 |
| Subscription to a CD-ROM database | = | $    900 per year |
| Subscription to a CD-ROM database for nonprint materials | = | $    900 per year |
| Smart barcode production software | = | $    250 |
| Total | = | $ 8,305 |

# Cost Estimate for Conversion by a Paraprofessional

To reduce the cost, a paraprofessional may be trained to conduct the conversion. The cost estimate would be:

| Hourly rate (salary) | = | $7 |
|---|---|---|
| Average number of minutes to convert, edit, enhance an item, and generate a barcode | = | 10 minutes |
| Number of minutes needed = 5,000 x 10 | = | 50,000 minutes |
| Number of hours needed = 50,000/60 | = | 833 hours |
| Labor cost = 833 x $7 | = | $ 5,831 |
| Subscription to a CD-ROM database | = | $    900 per year |
| Subscription to a CD-ROM database for nonprint materials | = | $    900 per year |
| Smart barcode production software | = | $    250 |
| Total | = | $ 7,881 |

Converting records without the use of a CD-ROM database is not recommended because creating a great number or records after the cataloging database is implemented is extremely time-consuming and increases both the cost of labor and the number of errors.

# BIBLIOGRAPHIC STANDARDS

The format and content of a database must be based on recognized bibliographic standards (i.e., MARC 21, *AACR2R*, and ISBD). The MARC standard is used to identify, store, and communicate cataloging information (Crawford 1989). The *Anglo-American Cataloguing Rules, Second Revised Edition (AACR2R)* (Gorman and Winkler 1988) consists of a set of rules for describing various types of materials. The International Standard Bibliographic Description (ISBD) provides eight elements to use in describing all types of materials, as well as a system of punctuation among the elements. This book treats only MARC 21. For information about *AACR2R* and ISBD, refer to the *Concise AACR2R* by Michael Gorman (1989).

Adhering to standards eliminates redundant efforts and thereby reduces cataloging cost, especially in a resource-sharing environment.

## MARC 21

In the late 1960s, the Library of Congress developed the United States Machine-Readable Cataloging (U.S. MARC) for use with mainframe computers. The main purpose of the standard is to share automated cataloging among libraries and allow records to be transferred from one automated system to another.

In 1987, a group of book vendors and publishers established the Microcomputer Library Interchange Format (MicroLIF), a MARC-based standard for use in microcomputer-based automation systems. Because the standard did not conform to U.S. MARC, it was revised in 1991. The revised standard was named U.S. MARC/MicroLIF Protocol to reflect its full compatibility and conformity with U.S. MARC. In 1998, the U.S. MARC and U.S. MARC/MicroLIF standards became known as MARC 21—meaning MARC for the twenty-first century—after it was combined with the Canadian MARC (CAN/MARC). It is important to emphasize that MARC 21 is *not* a new format. It supersedes the most recent editions of the U.S. MARC and Can/MARC formats (Stewart 2000). A sample MARC 21 record for a book is displayed in Figure 5.1.

**Note:** Knowledge of *AACR2R* is a prerequisite for understanding the MARC record; for more information on the subject, refer to Gorman (1989). A detailed discussion of MARC 21 is beyond the scope of this book; for more information on the subject, refer to Furrie's guide (2000). This brief MARC 21 guide is also available in full text on the Web through the Library of Congress (http://lcweb.loc.gov/marc/umb).

## Components of a MARC 21 Record

The MARC 21 record has various components that describe a cataloged item in an automated system. Following is a description of the components of a MARC 21 record.

## Figure 5.1. Sample MARC 21 record for a book.

```
Leader               01041cam  2200265 a 4500
Control #            001       89048230 /AC/r91
Control # Identifier 003       DLC
DTLT                 005       19911106082810.9
Fixed Data           008       891101s1990    maua j     001 0 eng
LCCN                 010 ƀƀ ‡a     89048230 /AC/r91
ISBN                 020 ƀƀ ‡a 0316107514 :
                             ‡c $12.95
ISBN                 020 ƀƀ ‡a 0316107506 (pbk.) :
                             ‡c $5.95 ($6.95 Can.)
Cat. Source          040 ƀƀ ‡a DLC
                             ‡c DLC
                             ‡d DLC
LC Call No.          050 00 ‡a GV943.25
                             ‡b .B74 1990
Dewey No.            082 00 ‡a 796.334/2
                             ‡2 20
ME:Pers Name         100 1ƀ ‡a Brenner,Richard J.,
                             ‡d 1941-
Title                245 10 ‡a Make the team.
                             ‡p Soccer :
                             ‡b a heads up guide to super soccer! /
                             ‡c Richard J. Brenner.
Varient Title        246 30 ‡a  Heads up guide to super soccer
Edition              250 ƀƀ ‡a 1st ed.
Publication          260 ƀƀ ‡a Boston :
                             ‡b Little, Brown,
                             ‡c c1990.
Phys Desc            300 ƀƀ ‡a 127 p. :
                             ‡b ill. ;
                             ‡c 19 cm.
Note: General        500 ƀƀ ‡a "A Sports illustrated for kids book."
Note: Summary        520 ƀƀ ‡a  Instructions for improving soccer skills.
                             Discusses dribbling, heading, playmaking,
                             defense, conditioning, mental attitude,
                             how to handle problems with coaches,
                             parents, and other players, and the
                             history of soccer.
Subj:Topical         650 ƀ0 ‡a  Soccer
                             ‡v Juvenile literature.
                     650 ƀ1 ‡a  Soccer.
```

## Leader

A Leader (LDR) consists of the first twenty-four characters that appear in most re-cords. The Leader encodes information that designates the length of a record, the status of a record (e.g., new, deleted, corrected, revised), and the type of record (e.g., book, serial, com-puter file, kit, sound recording). The Leader should be verified and revised by the cataloger as necessary. An interpretation of the Leader for the item in Figure 5.1 is provided below.

01041cam   2200265  a  4500

| 01041 | = The length of the record (in this case, it is 1041 characters). |
|---|---|
| c | = This record has been corrected or revised. |
| a | = This record is for printed material. (This is the default value.) If this record was for a kit, for example, the value would be **o** instead of **a**. |
| m | = This record is for a monograph. If this record was for a periodical, for example, the value would be **s** instead of **m**. |
| 2 | = Indicator count (always set at 2). |
| 2 | = Indicator count for subfield code (always set at 2). |
| 00 | = Base address of data (calculated for each record). |
| 263 | = This record occurs at character 263. |
| a | = This record is based on *AACR2R* cataloging. If the record was a CIP cataloging, for example, the value would be **8** instead of **a.** |
| 4 | = Length of the "length-of-field" portion (always 4). |
| 5 | = Length of the "starting-character-position" portion (always 5). |
| 0 | = Length of the "implementation-defined" n portion (always 0). |
| 0 | = Undefined position (always 0). |

The main values a cataloger may need to supply (for original cataloging) or verify (for records ordered from vendors) are those relating to the general type of the item cataloged (print or nonprint), record status (e.g., new, corrected, revised), and the kind of item cata-loged (e.g., monograph, kit, computer file). Most automated systems supply the rest of the information automatically. This is done after the automated system is implemented. It is not done on paper; it is performed in the cataloging module after the automation software has been installed and tested for proper operation. Some automation software packages, such as Follett Circ/Cat, allow the cataloger to select the type of material being cataloged from a menu, then the software itself supplies all the values for the Leader.

## Fixed Field (Tag 008)

The term *fixed field* is widely used to refer to the MARC tag 008. It describes the work cataloged (e.g., book, serial, software; its language; other details) and manages information retrieval by limiting results to material type, grade level, publication date, and other param-eters. The field is called a fixed field because it embraces codes (i.e., letters and numbers) rather than textual information and because it does not vary in length. Codes in this field vary from one cataloged item to another. An interpretation of the fixed field for the item in Figure 5.1 follows.

Fixed Data     008     891101s1990   maua   j  001 0  eng

008   = Tag for the fixed field.

89    = CIP cataloging was created in 1989.

1101  = The record was entered on November 1.

s     = The item has a single publication date.

1990  = The item was published in 1990.

mau   = Where the item was published (in this case, Massachusetts, United States).

a     = The item has illustrations.

j     = Target audience (the item is for *juvenile* audience).

001   = The first 0 means the item is not a conference publication, the second 0 means the item is not a Festschrift, the first number 1 means the item has an index.

0     = Not fiction.

eng   = The item is in the English language.

These values (codes) change based on the item being cataloged. If not present in a record, they must be supplied by the cataloger. A good source for finding these codes is the Library of Congress Web site (http://lcweb.loc.gov).

## *Variable Fields*

There are two types of variable fields: variable control fields and variable data fields.

### Variable Control Fields (Tags 001-009)

Variable control fields include tags 001 (control number), 005 (date and time of last transaction), 007 (physical description fixed field, i.e., physical characteristics of an item in code form), 008 (fixed field), and 009 (local use field). These fields do not have indicators or subfield codes and contain information expressed through the use of codes. (Indicators and subfield codes are defined later in this section.)

### Variable Data Fields (Tags 010-900)

Variable data fields include tags 010 (Library of Congress control number), 020 (International Standard Book Number), 022 (International Standard Serial Number), 040 (cataloging source), 041 (language code), 050 (Library of Congress call number), 092 (Dewey Decimal call number), 090 (local call numbers; it has been replaced by tag 900), and tags 100s to 900 (Furrie 2000). Variable data fields contain information expressed in text rather than code. They are called variable data fields because they vary in length and they contain indicators and subfield codes. (Indicators and subfield codes are defined later in this section.)

## *Local Field (Tag 900)*

The local field, indicated by tag 900, is reserved for local information (e.g., call number, barcode number, vendor information, price).

## *Tags*

Each variable field in a record (e.g., author, title, series) is identified by a three-digit code called a tag. The tag tells the computer what kind of information is contained in a particular field. Tag 100, for example, is reserved for an item's personal author main entry; tag 245 is reserved for its title and statement of responsibility.

Figure 5.2 lists general tags and field names in the hundreds series, and Figure 5.3 lists the most frequently used tags.

### Figure 5.2. General MARC 21 tags and field names in the 100s.

| Tag | Field Name |
| --- | --- |
| 0XX | Variable control fields |
| 1XX* | Main entry |
| 2XX | Title and statement of responsibility |
| 3XX | Physical description |
| 4XX* | Series statement |
| 5XX | Notes |
| 6XX* | Subject added entries |
| 7XX* | Author or title added entries |
| 8XX* | Series added entries |
| 9XX | Local field (e.g., local call number, barcode number, price, vendor information, etc.) |

*These fields require authority control.

### Figure 5.3. Most frequently used MARC 21 tags.

| | |
| --- | --- |
| 010 | LCCN |
| 020 | ISBN |
| 100 | Personal name main entry |
| 245 | Title proper and statement of responsibility |
| 250 | Edition (or version number of a computer file, a map's scale, etc., as applicable) |
| 260 | Publication information |
| 300 | Physical description |
| 440 | Series |
| 500 | Notes (e.g., general note, index, references) |
| 520 | Annotation or summary |
| 650 | Topical subject heading (Repeatable field) |
| 700 | Personal name added entry (Repeatable field) |
| 800 | Series added entry |
| 856 | URL address (Repeatable field) |
| 900 | Local field (e.g., local call number, barcode number, price, vendor information) |

## Indicators

Associated with each tag are two positions (or digits) reserved to further describe the contents of the field. For example, in the name field, the name may be just a first name, and the indicators relate to the formats of these entries. Indicators apply tags 100s, 200s, 400s, 500s, 600s, 700s, and 800s. Indicators appear as Arabic numerals next to a field tag.

Indicators vary from one field to another, according to the rules of the MARC 21 standard. For example, indicators in the personal name entry field (tag 100) vary with the type of name:

| | |
|---|---|
| 0 | for a forename only (no last name is used). Example: Cher. |
| 1 | for a single surname. Example: Asimov, Isaac. |
| 1 | for a multiple or hyphenated surname. Examples: De Mornay, Rebecca; Louis-Dreyfus, Julia. |
| 30 | For a family name. Example: The Benson's. |

**Note:** The indicator 20 that was used for a multiple/hyphenated surname became obsolete and was replaced by the indicator 1 (formerly 10) (Furrie 2000). The indicator in the title field has two digits. The first digit is reserved for making a title added entry, as applicable. The second digit is reserved for filing the title based on the initial articles appearing in the beginning of the title, as applicable. Indicators in the title field (tag 245) vary depending on whether

An item has a main entry in tag 100,

An item does not have a main entry in tag 100,

An item begins with an initial article, or

An item does not begin with an initial article.

*An item has a main entry in tag 100.* When an item has a main entry in tag 100, the first indicator digit in tag 245 (title and statement of responsibility) is 1. This indicates to the computer that a title added entry is needed. This is illustrated in the following example:

| Tag | Indicator | Main Entry |
|---|---|---|
| 100 | 1 | Bilal, Dania. |
| **Tag** | **Indicator** | **Title** |
| 245 | 1 | *Automating media centers and small libraries.* |

*An item does not have a main entry in tag 100.* When an item does not have a main entry in tag 100, the first indicator digit is 0 (zero) because the title becomes the main entry (based on *AACR2R*). Following is an example:

| Tag | Indicator | Main Entry |
|---|---|---|
| 100 | - | - |
| **Tag** | **Indicator** | **Title** |
| 245 | 0 | *Library research made easy.* |

*An item has a main entry and a title that begins with an initial article.* When the title of an item has a main entry and its title begins with an initial article, the second indicator digit in tag 245 indicates the number of characters in the initial article (e.g., a, an, the) *plus* a single space. This tells the computer to ignore the article (plus one space) when filing a record by title. As illustrated in the example below, four characters must be ignored in filing *The librarian and reference queries:* three characters for the word *The* and one for the space following it. The digit 1 indicates that the title should be an added entry.

| Tag | Indicator | Main Entry |
|-----|-----------|------------|
| 100 | 1 | Jahoda, Gerald. |
| Tag | Indicator | Title |
| 245 | 14 | *The librarian and reference queries.* |

*An item without a main entry begins with an initial article.* When the title of an item does not have a main entry and its title begins with an initial article, the first digit in the indicator is 0 and the second digit depends on the number of initial articles to be ignored in filing the title, plus one space. The title in the example below does not have a main entry, and its title begins with the initial article *An.* Thus, the indicator in tag 245 becomes 03 (the 0 for not having a main entry and the 3 for ignoring two initial articles [*An*] plus one space in filing the title).

| Tag | Indicator | Main Entry |
|-----|-----------|------------|
| 100 | - | - |
| Tag | Indicator | Title |
| 245 | 03 | *An introduction to the Web.* |

Indicators must also be applied to author added entries (tags 700s) and series (tags 800s). To find these indicators, use the MARC guide by Furrie (2000).

## Subfield Codes

Each field may be divided into subfields. A field may have one, two, three, or more subfields. The value of a field varies within its subfields and from one field to another. The publication field (tag 260), for example, contains three subfields; they indicate the place of publication, publisher, and publication date and bear the values a, b, and c, respectively. The following example is pulled from Figure 5.1.

| Tag | Delimiter and Subfield Code | Content of Field |
|-----|------------------------------|------------------|
| 260 | _a | Boston: |
|  | _b | Little, Brown |
|  | _c | c1990. |

## *Delimiters*

Each subfield code is preceded by a special symbol called a delimiter. (In the preceding example, the delimiter is _.) A delimiter varies from one MARC record to another, depending on the automated system in place. A delimiter may appear as a double dagger (††), a dollar sign ($), an underscore (_), or in another form. Whatever its form, the delimiter appears before each subfield code.

Because tags, indicators, and subfield codes identify each element in a bibliographic record, they are known as *content designators*. Values for all components of a MARC record can be found in the MARC manual by Furrie (2000).

## *Anglo-American Cataloguing Rules, Second Revised Edition (AACR2R)*

*Anglo-American Cataloguing Rules* are based on a set of standard rules for describing various types of materials. Published in 1967, the rules were revised in 1978 "to bring together separate North American and British texts of 1967 . . . and to reorganize and express the rules in a simpler and more direct way" (Gorman 1989, vii). The rules were revised again in 1988; at that time they became known as *AACR2R* (Gorman and Winkler 1988). Adherence to the rules is important for maintaining consistency in cataloging and for providing effective information retrieval.

## International Standard Bibliographic Description (ISBD)

ISBD is a standard that provides eight elements of a description for various types of materials and a system of punctuation among the elements. The elements, called areas, follow:

> Title and Statement of Responsibility Area
>
> Edition Area
>
> Special area for serials, computer files, maps and other cartographic materials, and music Area Publication, Distribution, etc., Area
>
> Physical Description Area
>
> Series Area
>
> Note Area
>
> Standard Number Area

# BARCODING THE COLLECTION

Barcoding is the process of placing a barcode on each item in the database. A barcode identifies a specific item and allows it to be checked in and out by using a barcode scanner or by keying the barcode number into the automated system.

# Barcodes

A barcode contains both bars and spaces. A row of numbers (up to fourteen digits) appears under the code to indicate the meaning of the bars and spaces. There are two main barcode standards: Codabar and Code 39 (Saffady 1999). Within these standards, there are various types of barcode symbology or format; for example, in Code 39 are the types Mod 10, Mod 11, and Mod 13. As seen in Figure 5.4, a Code 39 Mod 10 barcode has four components: type indicator or barcode type (e.g., patron, item); location code; identification number (e.g., of an item or patron); and a check digit, which verifies the accuracy of the barcode during scanning. Patron barcodes must be distinguished from material barcodes. Barcodes that start with the number 1 may be assigned to patrons, for example, and those that begin with the number 2 may be assigned to materials.

**Figure 5.4. Code 39 Mod 10 barcode.**

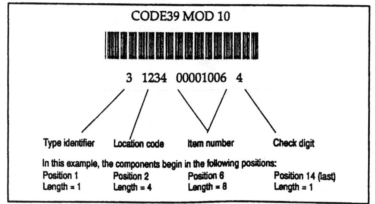

Reprinted with permission from Follett Software Company, *Library Automation Solutions Reference Guide* (McHenry, IL: Follett Software Company, 2000).

Barcodes can be either smart or dumb. Smart barcodes are linked to their respective items during recon. A smart barcode identifies its respective item without scanning it in the automated system (i.e., by looking at it) because it contains the item's title, call number, and author in addition to the name of the institution. Dumb barcodes are generic; they do not identify any items' titles, call numbers, or authors until they are linked to their respective items in the automated system. Generic barcodes usually bear the name of the institution only. Linking dumb barcodes to their respective items may be performed as materials are cataloged, converted, or on-the-fly (i.e., during check-out).

# Acquiring Barcodes

Barcodes are acquired through a vendor or are generated in-house using a barcode production software package that is compatible with an existing automated system. A few automated systems have barcode generator software (e.g., Sagebrush Corporation). Before making a decision to purchase barcodes or generate them in-house, perform a cost analysis to determine the most cost-effective method.

Barcodes must be compatible with the automated system in place. Before ordering barcodes, develop specifications for them and keep them on file. You may specify that each smart barcode should include the name of the media center or library, the item's call number and author, and other information you determine is useful. Barcodes must also be durable, easy to scan, and have a protective coating (Beiser 1999). Keep the barcode range on file so each time additional barcodes are ordered, the barcodes are kept in correct sequence.

## Procedures for Barcoding the Collection

Barcoding is a very time-consuming process. The larger the collection, the more time it will take to barcode it. The availability of adequate staffing and the development of a good plan may reduce barcoding time. For example, before the process begins, it must be determined which materials will be barcoded. For example, will materials in the vertical file be barcoded?

Following are procedures that may facilitate barcoding:

- Make an effort to close the media center or library to the public to avoid interruption and to expedite the process.

- Recall checked-out items.

- Divide the shelves into sections, and barcode one section at a time. If adequate staffing is available, one or more staff members may be given responsibility for barcoding one or more sections.

- Use the smart barcodes first, because they are arranged by call numbers and, possibly, by prefixes (e.g., fiction, biographies).

- Verify each item's call number against the call number on the barcode. If the call numbers match, place the barcode on the item in the designated area. (See the section below about placing barcodes.) Make sure all smart barcodes have respective items in the collection.

During barcoding, you may encounter errors in barcode labels (e.g., in call numbers or titles) and find that several barcodes are missing. If these or other problems occur, contact the vendor for replacement. If this problem is detected for barcodes generated in-house, then the barcodes will have to be regenerated.

## Protecting Barcodes

Scanning barcodes causes them to deteriorate over time unless they are laminated or covered with protectors. In addition, barcodes are subject to vandalism. Make sure that barcodes are safeguarded against both types of damage. If the barcode labels have good protectors, then users will find them hard to remove.

## Placing Barcodes on Print Materials

Where on the item a barcode is placed is determined by how items are scanned during inventory and by the type of material (e.g., print, audio disc, videotape) being barcoded. To choose the best placement, first simulate the collection inventory process by selecting sample items to scan. Determine the barcode placement that will make scanning easiest and fastest.

Following are some of the many options for barcoding print materials:

- Place the barcode on the front book cover in the top right or top left corner, vertically or horizontally.

- Place the barcode on the outside of the back cover in the top right or top left corner, vertically or horizontally.

- Place the barcode inside the back cover in the top right or top left corner, vertically or horizontally.

- Place the barcode inside the front cover in the top right or top left corner, vertically or horizontally.

- Place two identical barcodes, one inside and one outside the cover, in the top right or top left corner, vertically or horizontally. If the media center or library cannot afford purchasing two barcodes per item, staff may place one barcode in the preferred area and transcribe the barcode number inside the item using a permanent marker.

- Avoid placing a barcode on an item's spine or where important information will be covered.

## Barcoding Electronic Materials

Barcoding electronic materials, such as CD-ROMs, audiotapes, videocassettes, audio discs, laser discs, DVD, and computer software, requires careful consideration because barcode scanning may damage the encoded information.

Most electronic materials are multipart items because they include accompanying pieces (e.g., guides, manuals, booklets). Recommendations for barcoding these materials follow:

- Place a barcode on the outside of an item's container, cover, or jacket, preferably in the upper left corner.

- Transcribe the barcode number on each accompanying piece (e.g., booklet, guide) using a permanent marker.

- Label each accompanying item above or below the barcode number to alert circulation staff that the item is part of a set.

- Transcribe the barcode number on the item's label using a permanent marker.

# SUMMARY

Significant developments in the automation marketplace have taken place in recent years and have had an impact on how media specialists or information professionals will prepare their collections for retrospective conversion. Fee-based Web services for recon and Web services have made MARC records available for access and download at no cost. Although these services have advantages, media specialists or information professionals must be aware of the problems they may encounter in using Web-based services. Slow Web access, corruption of MARC records during electronic transfer (FTP), inability to import records into a local automated system, and errors in cataloging and in application of the MARC standard are critical issues. In making a decision about the method(s) to choose for recon, media specialists or information professionals should assess the pros and cons of each method discussed in this chapter against goals and needs of their media centers or libraries.

Collection preparation can be tedious and time-consuming. Many decisions must be made at this stage, especially with regard to weeding and inventorying the collection, standardizing the shelflist, and identifying the part of the collection that is the subject for recon. Regardless of the recon method you choose, develop specifications for this process and keep it on file. These specifications will provide a means for assessing the quality of MARC records. They will not only guide the recon process but may also be used when purchasing MARC records from book vendors.

Preparing the collection involves barcoding each item converted into a MARC format so that it can be checked out, checked in, and inventoried using an inventory device. Before barcoding the collection, make decisions about barcode placement on print and nonprint materials. Performing these collection activities should prepare you to undertake the next steps in system implementation (i.e., site preparation, software installation and testing, user training, and database management), which are described in Chapter 6.

# REFERENCES

Beiser, Karl. 1999. Integrated library system software for smaller libraries. Part 2. School, academic, and public libraries. *Library Technology Reports* 35 (4): 365-548.

Book Systems. 2000. EZCat/Pro. Available: http://www.booksys.com/ezcatpro/maininfo.html. (Accessed October 29, 2001).

Crawford, Walt. 1989. *MARC for library use*. Boston: G. K. Hall.

Follett Software Company. 2000. *Library automation solutions reference guide*. McHenry, IL: Follett Software Company.

Furrie, Betty. 2000. *Understanding MARC bibliographic: Machine-readable cataloging*. Washington, DC: Library of Congress. Also available at http://lcweb.loc.gov/marc/umb. (Accessed October 29, 2001).

Gorman, Michael. 1989. *The concise AACR2R: 1988 revision*. Chicago: American Library Association.

Gorman, Michael, and Paul Winkler. 1988. *Anglo-American cataloguing rules, second revised edition*. Chicago: American Library Association.

Saffady, William. 1999. *Introduction to automation for librarians*. 4th ed. Chicago: American Library Association.

Stewart, Margaret. 2000. MARC harmonization update: Part 1. Background to MARC 21. Available: http://www.fis.utoronto.ca/people/affiliated/tsig/stewart.html. (Accessed October 29, 2001).

## *Activity: Cost Analysis for Recon*

**Objective:** To perform a cost analysis for recon of a specific media center or library collection.

**Description**

1. Select a media center or a library for which you would like to do a cost analysis for recon.

2. Determine the size of the collection, including print and nonprint materials.

3. Contact three recon vendors to determine what they charge to convert each item in the collection, including the cost of enhancement per item (e.g., field 521, 856). This contact may be by phone, e-mail, or via the vendors' Web sites.

4. Contact three main software vendors who provide MARC databases on CD-ROM. Give the size of MARC records contained in each database. Give the subscription cost of each database (print and nonprint items) for one year. This contact may be by phone, e-mail, or by accessing the vendors' Web sites.

5. Access three fee-based Web services that provide recon via the Web. Give the names of these. Determine the cost of the service provided and its nature (e.g., search, edit, save, download, import).

6. Calculate the estimated cost of both vendor and in-house conversion (using both CD-ROM databases and Web-based services) based on the cost analysis methods provided in this chapter.

7. Describe which recon method(s) you would adopt and state the reasons why.

# Chapter 6

## Implementing the Automated System

    The implementation of the automated system involves site preparation (selection and placement of computer stations, printers, and furniture), installation and testing of the software, creation of patron records, system maintenance and security, training, evaluation of system use, and database maintenance.

    In implementing the automated system, one must not underestimate the importance of the "human factor." Staff and patrons will be the primary users of the new automated system and, therefore, their comfort levels and needs should be taken into consideration.

## SITE PREPARATION: SELECTION AND PLACEMENT OF HARDWARE

    If the new automated system will run on existing hardware, then a completely new computer facility need not be designed, but the location and arrangement of the existing computers may have to be rethought. When existing hardware is not already in place, planning the selection and placement of computer stations, printers, barcode scanners, furniture, and other equipment must be done in advance so that necessary hardware is available during system installation and testing.

### Computer Stations

    Two types of computer stations are needed for automated systems: lookup stations and administrative stations. Lookup stations are used by patrons to find information in the OPAC. The number of stations to acquire depends on an estimate of the number of users who will access the OPAC simultaneously and on the number of employees who will be assisting users and performing administrative tasks. One should also take into consideration whether the building where the media center or library is located is or will be wired to support a local area network (LAN). In a networked environment, access to the OPAC may be available from offices, computer laboratories, homes, or other locations.

The number of lookup stations depends on the number of users. One lookup station is recommended for 50 to 100 users. At least one computer station is needed to support circulation and information services functions, and another computer station is needed for administrative tasks (e.g., preparing statistics reports, overdue notices). The software vendor provides the minimum hardware specifications needed for lookup stations. All computer stations must be compatible with the automation software purchased. For this reason, they must meet the specifications established by the software vendor.

Lookup stations may be scattered throughout the media center or library or clustered in one or more locations to resemble a computer laboratory or study area. Stations should be placed close to staff to ensure that user assistance is readily available and to monitor system security.

## Printers

Printers allow OPAC users to print citations and generate bibliographies. They are also used to support administrative tasks. One printer is recommended for every five lookup stations. Another printer will be needed to support administrative tasks. Printers have plummeted in prices, and many media centers or libraries can afford reliable ones. Inkjet printers may be used for lookup stations and laser printers for administrative stations. The purchase of printers should be based on the recommendation of the software vendor and should be specified in your RFP for hardware.

## Furniture

Computer stations are usually placed on tables of various heights so that users may either sit or stand while using them. The height and size of tables and chairs may also depend on the age of the patrons. In an elementary school media center, for example, chair heights should be between 11 and 15 inches and the height of tables between 22 and 26 inches. The width of the tables should be between 54 and 60 inches and the depth between 24 and 36 inches. (For additional information, see Everhart 1998.) The department of education in your state may also have guidelines for furniture and other equipment.

When purchasing furniture, pay attention to all users, including those with special needs. Furniture, especially chairs, should be ergonomic and comfortable. Morris and Dyer (1998) stress the importance of "human factors" in automating a library. An automated system is designed for use by staff and patrons. If workstations are poorly designed, they can result in poor health and can induce or increase stress. Morris and Dyer maintain that "if people respond badly to the introduction of a new system, the anticipated effectiveness will not be achieved" (1998, xvi).

# INSTALLATION AND TESTING OF SOFTWARE

After retrospective conversion is completed and hardware and software are available, the automation software is installed and tested for proper operation. MARC records are downloaded and the database of bibliographic records is created. The circulation module will not include any patron records. The media specialist or information professional will create these records. More information about patron records is provided below.

Many problems may occur during and after installation. Failure to access one or more modules (such as the cataloging module or the circulation module) is one possible problem. Other problems may involve the use of peripherals, such as barcode scanners and printers. Testing the system thoroughly, including the use of all peripherals in all modules, is essential to ensure proper operation of the system, its software and hardware compatibility, and its conformity to the needs and requirements (or specifications) of the media center or library.

The automated system must not become available for use before all problems are worked out and staff are trained and proficient in using it. To become acquainted with the automated system during the testing period, catalog a few titles, enter selected patron records, circulate a few items, prepare purchase orders (in the acquisitions module), customize selected features (in the utilities module), and retrieve selected titles (in the OPAC module). Allow a minimum of one week for you and your staff to become familiar with the system. Software vendors usually offer a professional training program for a fee. It is recommended that you enroll in this program to become knowledgeable about the main features of operating the software.

## Patron Records

Creating patron records in the circulation module is time-consuming. Staff, students, and other clients must have circulation records containing their name, address, telephone number, social security number, homeroom number (for public schools), and other necessary information.

Many public schools have a database for maintaining student records. If the software package used for the database is compatible with the automated system, then student records can be imported into it. This activity will save a tremendous amount of time that would otherwise be spent on creating student records manually. Consult with the automated system vendor before you import any records into the circulation module so that you are assured that such activity would not corrupt your database.

# SYSTEM MAINTENANCE

## Environmental Care

Computers should be placed in areas where the air entering computer equipment does not exceed 80 percent relative humidity. High humidity can cause damage in metal contacts and circuits (Boss 1998). In placing computer stations, take into account direct sunlight, heat or draft, glare from windows, traffic patterns, and existing electrical wiring.

All hardware, including computer stations, servers, hubs, and devices supporting the operation of the LAN, should be located in a cool, clean, and secure area. The cabling system connecting the LAN should be covered with conduits to protect users from tripping over them and to avoid loss of data that could occur if the cables were inadvertently disconnected. The endpoint of the LAN cabling system and the hubs should be placed in a secure wiring closet away from users. Cables, wires, and computer stations should be isolated from moisture, mold, and water. Areas that are susceptible to flood (e.g., a basement) should not be considered for storing the LAN wiring closet, hubs, or other devices. Make sure you place servers in a safe and environmentally controlled room away from traffic and patron access. Some servers are supplied with an uninterruptible power supply (UPS) device to protect the system against blackouts, surges, and other problems. If the servers you purchase do not have such a device, you should purchase one and install it.

## System Backup

Every media center or library must develop a backup strategy for the automated system to recover from damaged data. Loss of data may occur due to hard disk crash, fire, theft, power outage, and accidental deletions. Having a backup plan will eliminate the need for re-entering the data. Backup can be done on a variety of hardware devices, including tapes, Zip or Jazz drives, recordable CDs, floppy diskettes, and secondary hard drives. Make sure you back up your data files daily and the entire system once a week. Keep the drives for the backups, label them, and store them in a safe place off-site. It is recommended that you use the automation software manual for instructions on how to back up the system and how to recover lost data.

## Security

Media centers and libraries must adopt security measures to prevent theft of library materials. One of these measures is to install a theft detection system. Boss (1998) lists two arrangements for these systems: a "full-circulation" model and a "by-pass" model. In the "full-circulation" model, security targets are deactivated as part of the check-out process. Patrons with checked-out materials can leave the library without setting off an alarm. The security targets are reactivated when materials are returned. In the "by-pass" model, patrons check-out materials and hand them to a staff member who passes them around the detection point, by-passing the sensors. "By-pass" systems are less expensive than "full circulation" systems. The top three leading suppliers of theft detection systems are 3M (http://www.3m.com/library), Check Point Systems, Inc. (http://www.checkpointsystems.com), and ID Systems (http://www.idsystems.com). For evaluation of security systems, use *Library Technology Reports*. The May-June 1999 issue, for example, contains a description of different types of security systems and evaluation of the systems supplied by five leading companies. Security personnel must monitor the media center or library facility on a regular basis to prevent theft, vandalism, and other problems.

Another security measure that must be taken concerns computers. Computer systems are vulnerable to breaches by computer hackers. Hackers may modify or destroy local files, inflict viruses, and break into remote systems. Therefore, media centers and libraries must adopt security measures to protect the software and hardware from serious harm. Measures may include firewalls to prevent unauthorized access from or to a LAN, virus protection software, and locking devices on computer stations. Table 6.1 lists several vendors of security systems and devices.

## Table 6.1.
## Selected Vendors of Security Systems and Devices

| Company | Address | Internet Address* |
|---|---|---|
| Brodart Library Supplies | P. O. Box 3037 Williamsport, PA 17705 (888) 820-4377 | http://www.brodart.com |
| Check Point Systems | 101 Wolf Dr. Thorofare, NJ 08086 (800) 257-5540 | http://www.checkpointsystems .com |
| Computer Security Products, Inc. | P. O. Box 7544 Nashua, NH 03060 (800) 466-7636 | http://www.ComputerSecurity .com |
| Gaylord Library Supplies | P. O. Box 4901 Syracuse, NY 13221 (800) 448-6160 | http://www.gaylord.com |
| Highsmith Company | P. O. Box 800 Fort Atkinson, WI 53538 (800) 558-2110 | http://www.hpress.highsmith .com |
| ID systems | 174 Concord St. Peterborough, NH 03458 (603) 924-9631 | http://www.idsystems.com |
| Innovative Security | 3904 W. 102 St. Overland Park, KS 66207 (913) 385-2002 | http://www.isecure.com |
| Sudanco | 3217 Crites St. Fort Worth, TX 76118 (800) 275-2824 | http://www.sudanco.com |
| 3M Worldwide | Building 224-2E-40 St. Paul, MN 55119 (800) 328-0067 | http://www.3m.com/library |

**\* URLs last accessed on October 29, 2001.**

# TRAINING

Every automated system, regardless of its simplicity, will require effective training to operate it properly. The extent of training to be provided varies among staff and patrons.

## Staff

Staff training should include all the modules in place, from utility to the OPAC. Staff should be involved in the professional training program provided by the software vendor. If it is costly to involve all staff members, however, it is advisable that a few staff members undergo the training and become in charge of training other staff members. Once staff become knowledgeable and skilled in using the automation software, they can be involved in training patrons.

## Patrons

Patrons are usually trained by staff who provide reference assistance. In a media center, the media specialist provides the training. Patrons may include students and teachers.

*Information Power* (AECT & AASL 1998) places information literacy skills at the heart of the nine standards for student learning. (An excerpt of these standards is located at http://www.ala.org/aasl/ip_nine.html.) Three standards describe what makes a student "information literate": effective and efficient access to information (Standard 1), evaluation of information critically and competently (Standard 2), and use of information accurately and creatively (Standard 3). These standards should be taken into consideration when designing information skills programs.

Training may take different forms: group presentation, individualized or self-paced, Web-based tutorial, and class-integrated. With the increased use of the Web in schools and other libraries, effective training programs for using the OPAC have become a necessity.

Research has shown that adults and children experience problems in using various OPACs. They accept search defaults even when many search options are available, are unable to formulate effective search strategies, have inadequate knowledge of how to use Boolean operators, and experience difficulties with information overload (Cooper 2001; Walter, Borgman, and Hirsh 1996; Borgman et. al. 1995; Solomon 1993; Chen 1993; Wallace 1993; Ensor 1992; Kuhlthau 1991; Edmonds, Moore, and Balcom 1990; Blazek and Bilal 1988).

There is no doubt that OPACs have revolutionized the way users access and retrieve information; the power of OPACs to search by author, title, subject, keyword, and Boolean logic far exceeds the search strategies that can be used with the card catalog. Web-based OPACs require training not only in maneuvering the OPAC but also in using a Web browser effectively and efficiently. Studies of children's use of the Web have shown that children possess naïve Web navigation skills and are not as successful in locating information as would be expected (Bilal 2001; Bilal 2000; Bilal 1998; Large and Beheshti 2000). These difficulties have serious implications for information literacy skills.

Teaching information literacy skills may be based on information literacy models, such as the Big6 Skills (Eisenberg and Berkowitz 1990), Pathways to Knowledge (Follett Software Company 1998), or Information Seeking Process (ISP) (Kuhlthau 1993). Providing effective information literacy programs will remedy deficiencies in information literacy skills and contribute to users' lifelong learning.

# OPACs ON THE WEB

All automation vendors will, eventually, provide a software package to interface OPACs with the Web. Making the OPAC available on the Web allows users to access your media center's or library's collection remotely. It will also provide an expanded access to the media center's or library's services. For additional information about this topic, see Chapter 9.

# EVALUATION OF SYSTEM USE

After the automated system has been implemented and staff and patrons have been trained, use of the system, including the OPAC, should be evaluated. Automated systems provide use statistics and reporting features. Circulation reports, for example, give an idea about collection use, collection age, peak transaction activity, and in-library use of materials. These reports may serve as an impetus for requesting increases in collection development funds and for scheduling additional staff during peak transaction hours.

Cataloging activity reports may identify deficiencies in MARC records, among other things. If MARC records obtained from certain vendors are deficient, for example, then a decision should be made to replace the vendor with a more reliable one. Cataloging errors may affect user information retrieval. Therefore, MARC records should be evaluated on a regular basis.

Statistics for use of the OPAC should also be assessed. For example, OPAC transactions can be collected to determine the total number of searches made daily, the number of successful and unsuccessful searches, the average and total OPAC log-in time, and the OPAC stations that are heavily used. Many decisions can be made based on these statistics. Examples are the type of OPAC training needed to increase successful searches, the time of the day during which additional staffing is needed to assist patrons in using the OPAC, and the location of the OPAC stations that receive the heaviest use (Everhart 1998).

# DATABASE MAINTENANCE

An automated system's database should reflect the status of items (e.g., existing, missing, lost, withdrawn). Circulation, cataloging, acquisitions, and interlibrary loan modules have records that should be maintained on a regular basis. Although maintaining record accuracy in every module is important, the cataloging module that stores MARC records should be given top priority, because it directly affects the ability of users to retrieve information.

Database cleanup has become vital with use of the Web, especially since many MARC databases are available for free access. Downloading records from these databases is becoming the "norm" in many libraries due to cost savings in cataloging. Web-based MARC services provide fast and economical means of obtaining MARC records, but many of them, especially those that are free of charge, contain errors and are problematic. Therefore, cleaning up MARC records is essential for maintaining the integrity of the bibliographic database. Database cleanup should also be performed after record conversion has been completed.

During the conversion, many errors and inaccuracies may have been committed, including mismatched records, incorrect indicators, incomplete fields, missing fields, inconsistent punctuation, and typographical errors. All of these errors and inconsistencies warrant database maintenance.

In media centers or libraries that are short staffed, database cleanup may not be a priority for media specialists or information professionals. It is noteworthy that such a task may be performed over a period of time and as time allows. As you encounter errors in the MARC database, print out the records requiring correction and place them in a box marked *Corrections*. Correct the errors at your earliest convenience.

In reviewing MARC records for cleanup, examine the Leader; fixed field; author fields; title field; subject fields; and alphabetical filing of author, title, and subject entries.

## The Leader

The main codes to examine in the Leader are those that pertain to the general type of material catalogued (i.e., print versus nonprint material) and the specific type of material (i.e., monograph, kit, computer file, printed music, projected medium, etc.). The accuracy of these codes is essential for limiting searches in OPAC by material type and for generating printed lists of various types of materials. The latter may be used to present a statistical comparison of materials for the benefit of balancing the collection.

Following is an example of an error to correct in the Leader:

> 000   cam   2200193 a 4500

The code cam was assigned to a videorecording. The correct code for a projected medium, such as videorecording is **g** not a. The correct Leader is:

> 000   cgm   2200193 a 4500.

## Fixed Field (Tag 008)

The data elements in the fixed field (tag 008) are frequently overlooked by media specialists and information professionals. Codes in this field may be used to limit searches in the OPAC by publication date, country name, audience level, language, and other characteristics. Frequently, MARC records have missing data in this field, such as date, city, and country of publication, among other information.

Following is an example of missing data to complete in tag 008:

008 s19**xx**   **xx**  a j 000 1 eng cam a.

Since the date of publication for this item is 1992, as indicated in tag 260 of its MARC record, the **19xx** should be **1992**. The **xx** code following this date reflects the city and country of publication of the item. It was published in New York, so the code should read **nyu** (New York, United States). The correct 008 is:

008 s1**992**   **nyu**  a j 000 1 eng cam a.

## Author Fields (Tag 100s)

Author field tag 100 is reserved for a personal author main entry. There are two elements to consider in this tag: the correct entry of an author name (i.e., single last name versus forename) and the indicator. The indicator instructs the system about how to file a name in a correct alphabetical order. Various indicators for this field are shown in Table 6.2.

## Table 6.2.
## Indicators in the Author Field (Tag 100)

| Type of Personal Name | Example | Indicator (Tag 100) |
|---|---|---|
| Forename only | Cher. | 0 |
| Forename and surname | Blume, Judy. | 10 |
|  | Maupassant, Guy de. | 10 |
| Surname and a word | Seuss, Dr. | 10 |
| Multiple surname | De Mornay, Rebecca. | 10 |
| Hyphenated surname | Williams-Ellis, Annabel. | 10 |
| Family name | The Kennedys. | 30 |

Another area to consider in main entry fields is the elimination of duplicate entries for identical names. An entry that ends with a period and an identical one that does not end with a period will appear as two separate entries in OPAC. Duplication will occupy disk space and cause confusion for the user. Based on *AACR2R*, all types of main entries (in tags 100s) must end with a period.

Following is an example of an error to correct in the indicator code for tag 100:

    100    00    Grimm Brothers.

This item is assigned an incorrect indicator. The correct indicator for a family name is 30. The correct indicator is:

    100    **30**    Grimm Brothers.

## Title Field (Tag 245)

The indicator associated with the title field (tag 245) does two things: It indicates to the automated system whether to make the title an added entry, and it instructs the computer about how to file a title. Various indicators applicable to this field are listed in Table 6.3.

If your automated system maintains a list of stop words of initial articles and automatically ignores non-filing characters, you will have to apply the correct indicator to the first digit only. Errors occur in filing records by title when the indicators in tag 245 are incorrect. (Refer to Chapter 5, the section on MARC 21, for the rules to apply to the indicator field in tag 245.) Remember that before you fill the indicator in tag 245, you must examine tag 100 or 110 or 130, as applicable.

Following is an example of an error to correct in the indicator for the title field:

    245    **04**    The big book for the planet.

## Table 6.3.
## Indicators in the Title Field (Tag 245)

| Main Entry (Tag 100) | Title (Tag 245) | Initial Article | Added Entry | Indicator |
|---|---|---|---|---|
| Carroll, Lewis. | The hunting of the snark | The | Yes | 14 |
| Hugo, Victor. | Les miserables | Les | Yes | 14 |
| None* | The ALA glossary of library | The | No | 04 |
| Bigham, Dane. | Where in the world is Carmen | None | Yes | 10 |
| Boyer, Carl B. | A history of mathematics | A | Yes | 12 |

*This item has no main entry.*

This item has an author (tag 100). Therefore, the title of the item should become an access point. This means that the first digit of the indicator field should be a 1 rather than a 0. Adding the digit 1 indicates to the computer to make an access point for the title; otherwise, this item will not be retrieved under its title.

The correct indicator for tag 245 is:

245    14    The big book for the planet.

## Subject Headings Fields (Tag 600s)

Many MARC records do not contain subject added entries. These records will minimize user information retrieval. If you encounter records that are missing these entries, add them based on *Sears List of Subject Headings* or another list you are using. Another problem in this field relates to use of incorrect tags for various subject headings. The correct tags to use are 600 (personal name subject heading), 610 (corporate name subject heading), 650 (topical subject headings), and 651 (geographic name subject heading). The various subdivisions of subject headings (i.e., form, general, chronological, and geographic) have their own subfield codes. Make sure you apply the correct codes to these headings.

Duplicate entries for subject headings are also problematic. Duplication occurs when one heading ends with a period and its identical one does not. You should merge these headings.

Following is an example of an error in the subject field (tags 650 and 651):

650    _aUnited States
       _xHistory.

The correct tag for this subject heading should be 651 instead of 650 because the subject heading is for a geographic name. All subjects about the history of the United States should begin with the heading United States.

The correct tag for the subject heading is:

651    _aUnited States
       _xHistory.

## Added Entry Fields (Tags 700s-800s)

Indicators for tag 700 (personal name added entry), 710 (corporate name added entry), 740 (related or variant title added entry), 800 (personal name series added entry), and 830 (uniform title series added entry) require verification. Consult Furrie's (2000) MARC manual for the appropriate indicators.

# SUMMARY

Implementation of the automated system is the fifth activity to undertake in completing the automation project. The first four activities to achieve are planning for automation, choosing a hardware configuration, selecting the automation software, and preparing the collection.

In implementing the automation system, staff who are in charge of the automation project must assess the appropriateness of the existing facility to determine placement of computer stations, printers, furniture, and other equipment. Having an automated system in place requires use of lookup stations for the OPAC and computer stations for administrative use. Hardware must adhere to the software vendor's specifications to ensure proper operation of the automated system. Lookup stations should be placed in proximity to staff so that user assistance is readily available and software and hardware can be observed for security.

Software installation should be followed by a thorough testing of the automated system to ensure hardware and software compatibility and the system's conformity to the media center's or library's specifications. A bibliographic database is created after MARC records are imported into the cataloging module. A patron database is created after patron information is input or imported into the system. When the system becomes fully operational, back up your data daily and the whole system weekly. Having a backup plan will eliminate the need for re-entering data lost due to blackouts, surges, natural disasters, or other problems.

Computers and other hardware devices should be placed in areas where the air entering the hardware does not exceed 80 percent humidity. Dehumidifiers may be necessary to maintain adequate moisture control. To protect your system, have a security plan in place. Installing firewalls, virus protection software, and theft protection systems will reduce unauthorized use, protect software, and minimize theft.

Staff and patrons should be trained in using the automated system. Staff should be knowledgeable about using all modules in the system, whereas patrons should be knowledgeable about using the OPAC. Information literacy skills programs should include patron training in using the Windows and Web interfaces of the OPAC effectively.

Database maintenance should be performed after the bibliographic database is created and any time new MARC records are added to the database. The database of patron records should also be maintained regularly.

# REFERENCES

AECT & AASL. 1998. *Information power: Building partnerships for learning*. Chicago: American Library Association.

Bilal, Dania. 1998. Children's search processes in using World Wide Web search engines: An exploratory study. *Proceedings of the 61ˢᵗ ASIS Annual Meeting, 35, October 24-29. Pittsburgh*. Medford, NJ: Information Today, 45-53.

_____.2000. Children's use of the Yahooligans! Web search engine. II. Cognitive and physical behaviors on Research tasks. *Journal of the American Society for Information Science* 52 (2): 118-36.

_____.2001. Children's use of the Yahooligans! Web search engine. I. Cognitive, physical, and affective behaviors on fact-based tasks. *Journal of the American Society for Information Science* 51 (7): 646-65.

Blazek, Ron, and Dania Bilal. 1988. Problems in OPAC: A case study of an academic research library. *RQ* 28 (2): 169-78.

Borgman, Christine, et. al. 1995. Children's searching behavior on browsing and keyword searching online catalogs: The Science Library Catalog project. *Journal of the American Society for Information Science* 46 (9): 663-84.

Boss, Richard. 1998. Model technology plans for libraries. *Library Technology Reports* 34 (1): 9-109.

Chen, Shu-Hsien. 1993. A study of high school students' on-line catalog searching behavior. *School Library Media Quarterly* 22 (Fall): 33-40.

Cooper, Michael D. 2001. Usage patterns of a Web-based catalog. *Journal of the American Society for Information Science and Technology* 52 (2): 137-47.

Edmonds, Leslie, Paula Moore, and Kathleen Mehaffey Balcom. 1990. The effectiveness of an online catalog. *School Library Journal* 36 (October): 28-33.

Eisenberg, Michael. B., and Robert E. Berkowitz. 1990. *Information problem-solving: The Big6™ skills approach to library & information skills instruction*. Norwood, CT: Ablex.

Ensor, Pat. 1992. Knowledge level of users and nonusers of keyword and Boolean searching on an online public access catalog. *RQ* 32 (Fall): 60-74.

Everhart, Nancy. 1998. *Evaluating the school library media center*. Englewood, CO: Libraries Unlimited.

Follett Software Company. 1998. *Pathways to knowledge: Follett's information skills model*. McHenry, IL: Follett Software Company.

Furrie, Betty. 2000. *Understanding MARC bibliographic: Machine-readable cataloging*. Washington, DC: Library of Congress.

Kuhlthau, Carol C. 1991. Inside the search process: Information seeking from the user's perspective. *Journal of the American Society for Information Science* 42 (5): 367-71.

———. 1993. *Seeking meaning*: *A process approach to library and information services.* Norwood, CT: Ablex.

Large, Andrew, and Jamshid Beheshti. 2000. The Web as a classroom resource: Reactions from the users. *Journal of the American Society for Information Science* 51 (12): 1069-80.

Morris, Anne, and Hilary Dyer. 1998. *Human aspects of library automation.* 2d ed. Brookfield, VT: Gower.

Solomon, Paul. 1993. Children's information retrieval behavior: A case analysis of an OPAC. *Journal of the American Society for Information Science* 44 (5): 245-64.

Wallace, Patricia M. 1993. How do patrons search the online catalog when no one's looking? Transaction log analysis and implications for bibliographic instruction and system design. *RQ* 33 (Winter): 239-51.

Walter, Virginia, A., Christine L. Borgman, and Sandra G. Hirsh. 1996. The science library catalog: Springboard for information literacy. *School Library Media Quarterly* 24 (Winter): 105-9.

## *Activity: Database Maintenance*

**Objective:** To perform database maintenance on a media center's MARC database and to evaluate the quality of the database.

**Description 1:** Access SUNLINK (http://www.sunlink.ucf.edu) on the Web and review a set of MARC records in any database. SUNLINK is a Web-based union catalog of Florida public schools. Locate MARC records that need correction in the fields listed below.

- **Author field (Tag 100 or 110).** At random, find five records that need correction in the indicator field for either or both tags. Print each record. Highlight or circle the wrong indicator and write the correct one above or adjacent to it. Label each printed record Author Field Correction.

- **Title field (Tag 245).** At random, find five records that need correction in the indicator field for tag 245. Print each record. Highlight or circle the wrong indicator and write the correct one above or adjacent to it. Label each printed record Title Field Correction.

- **Subject fields (Tags in 600s).** At random, find five records that need correction in any of the 600s tags. Print each record. Highlight or circle the wrong indicator and write the correct one above or adjacent to it. Label each printed record Subject Field Correction.

- **Fixed field (Tag 008).** At random, find five records that need completion of missing data or errors in tag 008. Print each record. Highlight or circle the area for the missing data or errors. Complete the missing data or correct existing errors. Label each printed record Fixed Field Correction.

**Description 2:** In one or two pages, describe what you have learned about the quality of MARC records in SUNLINK. How will your experience with this project influence your future decisions in using free Web-based MARC services?

# Chapter 7

## Networking

"A network is a collection of computers and devices connected by communication channels that allows users to share data, information, hardware, and software with other users" (Shelly et. al. 2000, 9-27). Networking can increase the use of scarce resources, provide access to information outside a particular media center or library, and connect the media center or library to a worldwide audience via the Internet/Web. A network may consist of two computers or of a collection of computers that are connected from around the world, such as the Internet.

## TYPES OF NETWORKS

A network may include minicomputers, microcomputers, mainframes, or any combination of them. A network can be concentrated in one building or can spread out over several buildings close to one another in a local area network (LAN); it can spread over a larger geographic area in a metropolitan area network (MAN); or it can span across geographic boundaries in a wide area network (WAN). Links among computers and peripherals can be achieved with coaxial cable, fiber optics. twisted-pair wire, radio, or infrared waves. The latter is the case with wireless LANs (WLANs). The major differences among these types of networks are geographic range and the speed of the connections.

### LANs

A LAN may link offices, laboratories, and other facilities in one building or in buildings close to one another. The typical links among computers and peripherals in the network can be achieved with twisted-pair cable, fiber optics, and coaxial cable.

There are two popular types of LANs: peer-to-peer and client/server.

## *Peer-to-Peer Network*

In a peer-to-peer network, computers are connected to one another to share software (e.g., automation programs) and hardware (e.g., printers) without the use of a dedicated file server. Absence of a file server means that the operating system and application software must be installed on each computer, or peer, in the network. More than one computer in the network can share the peripherals (e.g., printer, scanner, fax machine); the other computers on the network share these devices. A peer-to-peer network is easy to install, inexpensive, and incurs low maintenance. Computers can be connected together using twisted-pair cable or coaxial cable. The Windows operating system and Macintosh operating system (Mac OS) include a peer-to-peer networking utility that allows one to set up a small peer-to-peer network. A peer-to-peer network, however, is not recommended for an environment with more than ten computers.

As the number of computers increases, the network's performance decreases. Although this is true for all types of networks, it is more evident in peer-to-peer LANs than in those that make use of a client/server.

## *Client/Server Network*

A client/server network is based on a client/server computing architecture in which one or more dedicated computers are called servers and other computers connected to the servers are called clients. Clients share certain processing tasks with the servers. A server may store files, databases, and other data. A server controls access to the hardware and software on the network. A client/server network may have more than one dedicated server, such as Web server, e-mail server, file server, and database server. Novell Netware, Microsoft Windows NT, and Mac OS are common operating systems for a client/server network.

The main advantage of a client/server network lies in its expandability; it can accommodate many computers without compromising performance. It also allows centralized administration of the LAN. The disadvantages of a network system are its complexity, cost of installation, frequent maintenance, and the need for dedicated machines to act as servers.

# Metropolitan Area Network (MAN)

A MAN serves as a backbone network that connects LANs in a city or region. It uses fiber optics, leased telephone lines (e.g., T-1, T-3), radio, or infrared transmission devices to connect LANs to a WAN.

# Wide Area Network (WAN)

A WAN can be a nationwide or worldwide network. Satellites are used to establish communications among nodes, or earth stations. Earth stations may be linked to one another by microwave devices, cables, fiber optics, or telephone lines. The Internet is an example of a WAN that connects users around the world. Chapter 9 discusses the Internet in more detail.

# CONNECTING NETWORKS

Networks can be connected by using various hardware devices, such as repeaters, hubs, bridges, routers, and gateways. Repeaters amplify or regenerate data signals to span longer distances. Hubs are devices that join computer communication lines that are together in a star topology network (see page 135). Hubs are called Multiple Access Unit (MAU) in a ring topology network (see page 135). Bridges convert data between networks that have different architecture and that have similar datalink protocols. Specialized bridges are available for converting Ethernet and token ring LANs. Routers forward data from one LAN to another or from a WAN to another. Gateways perform protocol conversion between different types of networks or applications (e.g., TCP/IP to Netware IPX/SPX and vice versa). For further information about network hardware devices, access Tech Encyclopedia at http://www. techweb.com and What Is?.Com at http://whatis.techtarget.com. Stallings's *Business Data Communications* (2001) is also a good source.

# NETWORK COMPONENTS

A network comprises three components: cabling, topology, and architecture and protocols.

## Network Cabling

There are three types of cabling systems: twisted-pair, fiber optics, and coaxial. Cabling design and installation are extremely important for the proper operation of a network. The proper type of network cabling to use depends on the hardware platform, network topology, and model chosen. Two cabling models are most common in media centers and libraries: the lab model, which consists of a cluster of computer workstations and a server, and the distributed model, which involves computer stations that are remote from the server.

Cabling requires a well-planned design and proper installation. Poor implementation of a cabling system can result in data loss or slow performance.

### *Twisted-Pair Cable*

Twisted-pair cable is used to support communication in telephone and networking systems. There are six categories of twisted-pair cable. Category 1 is used in a telephone system. Category 2 transmits data up to 1 MHz and, like Category 1 cable, it is not used in horizontal network cabling systems. Category 3 is typically used for voice and data transmission rates up to 10 Mbps (megabytes per second). Category 3 represents the minimum transmission performance acceptable for horizontal cabling systems. Category 4 is intended for use with voice and data transmission for up to 20 Mbps but is rarely used. Category 5, which is the minimum recommended level for networking, transmits data at a rate of over 150 Mbps. Category 6 transmits data at 1 Gbps (gigabytes per second). If you were to install twisted-pair cables today, you would want to use category 6, if possible.

There are two kinds of twisted-pair cable: unshielded twisted-pair (UTP) and shielded twisted-pair (STP). UTP is a small, lightweight cable used in telephone connections and most LANs. It is inexpensive and relatively easy to install, but it is susceptible to data loss due to electromagnetic interference (EMI) and crosstalk among wires. UTP has a limited bandwidth, signal attenuation. Attenuation is a measure of signal loss. It is usually expressed as db/100m (decibels/100 meters). A decibel is a unit of measurement of gain or loss at a certain frequency (Black Box Network Services 2000). STP uses UTP with shielding. Unlike UTP, STP is bulky and heavy but rugged and reliable. Its shield provides excellent protection against EMI and crosstalk among wires. It has a limited bandwidth, however, and is also sensitive to damage during installation. STP has the same transmission speed and signal attenuation as UTP.

## Fiber Optic Cable

Fiber optic cable is a small, lightweight cable with a large bandwidth. It provides excellent performance for high-volume traffic, has a transmission speed of more than 2 Gbps, and signal attenuation of more than 60 kilometers. The attenuation signal for fiber optic cables is measured as db/km (decibels/kilometers). Because it uses light to transmit signals, it is not subject to EMI. A fiber optic cable is less susceptible to damage during installation and has no grounding problems; however, it is more expensive than twisted-pair or coaxial cable and can be difficult to install and maintain.

## Coaxial Cable

Coaxial cable has been used for high-frequency telegraph, telephone, and television signals. A type of coaxial cable is used to connect computer networks. Coaxial cable transports much information because of its large bandwidth. It is sturdy, resistant to electromagnetic interference (EMI), and transmits data at a speed up to 500 Mbps. Coaxial cable is easy to install but bulky and relatively expensive. The major issue in using this type of cable is that it does not support a Fast Ethernet network; thus, Ethernet speed is limited to 10 Mbps.

See Table 7.1 for a comparison of various cabling options.

# Cable Installation

Because cables are vulnerable to interference from outside sources, special considerations such as the following must be taken into account when cables are installed:

- Avoid running cables through areas in which there is heating and cooling equipment.

- Cover the cables with conduits or channels to minimize the interference and to protect both users and cables.

- Terminate a cable at a junction box with the appropriate type of jack so that computer stations can be easily plugged into the network.

- Know where the existing electric, gas, bell, and alarm lines are located when drilling through a wall.

- Ensure that all cables meet all technical or standard specifications. Request the specifications from the company that is supplying your networking products.

- Employ certified technicians for cable installation.

## Table 7.1. Comparison of Cabling Options

| Criteria | Twisted-pair (STP) | Twisted-pair (UTP) | Coaxial | Fiber optics |
|---|---|---|---|---|
| Cost | Moderate | Low | Moderate | High |
| Data transmission | 155Mbps | 155Mbps+ | 500Mbps | 2Gbps |
| Typical distance | 100 meters | 100 meters | 1 kilometer (km) | 2 to 60 km* |
| EMI | Good | Poor | Good | Excellent |

**\*Varies with the type of fiber: multi-mode (2km); single mode (60km).**
**+Up to 1gbps for shorter distances (~25 km).**

## Telephone Connections

There are two types of telephone connections: dedicated and dial-up. Dedicated telephone lines are leased from a telephone or communications service company. Leased lines can be either analog or digital. Analog lines are like dial-up lines; they require a modem at both the sending and receiving ends. Digital leased lines use coaxial cable, twisted-pair cable, fiber optic cable, microwaves, or infrared (Shelly et al. 2000). A modem is needed at both the sending and receiving ends of the communication channel. The quality of the connection in a dial-up telephone line is usually lower than that of a dedicated line because a telephone company randomly selects the line to use for establishing the communication. Some of the digital leased telephone lines are described below.

### Integrated Services Digital Network (ISDN)

This type of leased line provides much faster transmission rates than a regular telephone line. An ISDN line requires use of an ISDN adapter at both the sending and receiving ends. There are two types of ISDN lines: Basic Rate Interface (BRI) and Primary Rate Interface (PRI). The BRI is generally designed for home use. It is faster than a regular modem connection; it transmits data up to 128 Kbps (kilobytes per second). The PRI is comparable in speed to a T-1 line; it transmits data up to 1.54 Mbps. An ISDN line is typically a dial-up service for BRI (Shelley et. al. 2000).

### Digital Subscriber Line (DSL)

A DSL line uses a standard twisted-pair cable. It has a higher transfer rate than an ISDN line. The Asymmetric Digital Subscriber Line (ADSL) receives data ranging from 1.54 Mbps to 8.45 Mbps (downstream) and sends data ranging from 128 Kbps to 640 Kbps (upstream). A DSL modem is required for a DSL or an ADSL line.

### T-Carrier Lines

T-carrier lines are digital telephone lines. The most popular of these is the T-1 line. It carries twenty-four separate channels at a transmission rate of 64 Kbps each for a total transmission rate of 1.54 Mbps. Another type of T-carrier line is T-3, which carries 672 individual channels at a transmission rate of 64 Kbps each, totaling the transmission rate at ~ 45 Mbps. T-3 lines are more expensive than T-1 lines. The cost of a T-carrier varies based on location (Shelley et al. 2000).

Another type of connection is Asynchronous Transfer Mode (ATM). ATM is a service offered by Local Exchange Carriers (e.g., Bell South, Ameritech) and by The Interexchange Carriers (e.g., AT&T, MCI). It can be used over T-1 and T-3 lines. ATM transmits voice, data, video, and multimedia over a single line at high speeds (622 Mbps or higher). It is used in telephone networks, the Internet, or networks with high traffic.

## Other Types of Connections

### Frame Relay

Frame Relay is a packet-switching protocol for connecting devices on a WAN at speeds up to 45 Mbps.

### Cable Modems

A cable modem is a hardware device that sends and receives data over the cable television infrastructure. It is ideal for home use where fast access to the Internet is needed. A cable modem transmits data at a speed ranging from 500 Kbps to 2 Mbps, much faster than an ISDN line (from 128 Kbps to 1.54 Mbps) and a standard modem (28K to 56K). Cable modem is a shared infrastructure; the more people that have it in a geographical area, the slower is the data transmission.

# NETWORK TOPOLOGY

Network topology, or the physical layout of the network, can be designed as a bus, star, or ring layout. Note that MANs typically use a ring topology.

## Bus Topology

A bus topology consists of computers connected by a single central cable (bus) through which the information passes to all computers and devices. It is often used with small LANs and peer-to-peer networks. This topology may be used with or without a server. Figure 7.1 shows a bus network without a server. It does not require a hub or concentrator for connecting the computers. Any computer or device can be disconnected from the network without affecting network performance. In addition, failure of one computer or device does not affect the rest of the network. Troubleshooting the network is problematic, however, because any malfunction in the central cable can disrupt communications across the entire network. Note that bus networks are typically wired as a star topology (the only option with twisted-pair cable). In this case, the bus is centrally implemented within the hub.

**Figure 7.1. Bus topology network.**

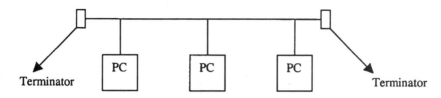

<## Star Topology>
## Star Topology

A star topology network consists of computers connected to a server that is linked to a hub or concentrator by cable or fiber optics to form a star (see Figure 7.2). Typically, all computers (PCs and servers) are connected to the hub. A star network can be used for a peer-to-peer LAN. More than one hub may be used to accommodate a high number of connections. Similarly, more than one server may be employed to serve high traffic. All data transmitted pass through the hub. Because the computers in the network are connected to a hub rather than to each other, cabling problems are isolated and easy to detect. This means that if one device in the network fails, the other devices are not affected, thus making troubleshooting easier. If the hub fails, however, the whole network becomes inoperable.

**Figure 7.2. Star topology network.**

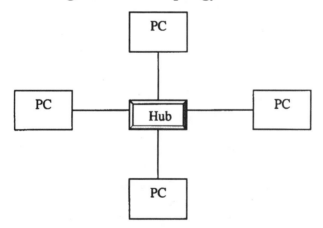

## Ring Topology

In a ring topology, computers and devices are arranged along a cable that forms a ring or loop (see Figure 7.3). Data pass from one device to another around the entire ring and in one direction until they reach their destination. Like the star network, one or more servers may be used. A hub called Multiple Access Unit (MAU) is employed. If a computer on the ring fails, all computers *before* the failed computer remain unaffected, but those *after* the affected computer become inoperable. Typically, a ring topology is wired as a star. The MAU is the central point of the star.

**Figure 7.3. Ring topology network.**

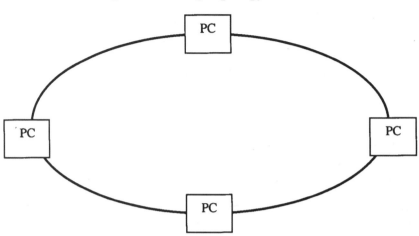

# NETWORK ARCHITECTURE

The three common network architectures or designs are Ethernet, token ring, and fiber distributed data interface (FDDI). The key factors to consider in choosing a network design are its purpose, existing and future applications, speed, reliability, security, ease of installation and maintenance, and cost.

## Ethernet Architecture

Ethernet is one of the oldest and most widely used protocols. Ethernet is based on the Institute of Electrical and Electronics Engineers (IEEE) Carrier-Sense Multiple Access/Collision Detection (CSMA/CD) 802.3 standard, an access-control technique that attempts to detect and recover from collisions. A computer that has data to send monitors the medium (carrier-sense). If the medium is idle, the computer transmits immediately but continues to monitor the medium for a collision. If a collision is detected, all computers that are transmitting cease immediately. Computers that have data to send will wait for a random period of time before attempting to transmit again.

Each computer station in an Ethernet network requires a network interface card (NIC). This is also true for the other two architectures. Ethernet operates over fiber optics, STP and UTP, and coaxial cable.

A baseband is a telecommunications system in which information is carried in digital form on a single signal channel on a transmission medium. There are four baseband schemes: ThinNet or 10Base2, which uses inexpensive coaxial cable and transmits data at 10 Mbps; Thick Ethernet or 10Base5, which transmits data at 10 Mbps and up to 500 meters in distance; 10BaseT, which uses a twisted-pair cable and transmits data at 10 Mbps; and 10BaseF, which use a fiber optic cable. The newest baseband schemes are Fast Ethernet, which transmits data at 100 Mbps, and Gigabit Ethernet, which transmits data at 1 Gbps. A 10 Gbps Ethernet is under development. Ethernet is reliable, inexpensive, and can be implemented with various topologies. The actual data transmission rate depends on the amount of traffic on the network.

## Token Ring Architecture

The token ring architecture uses a token-passing technology, which allows frames of data to be attached to the token. Only the device with the token can transmit data over the network; each message is sent to the next connected device until it reaches its destination (Comer 2001).

The token ring protocol is based on IEEE standard 802.5. It typically operates over STP and UTP at a speed of 4 Mbps using unshielded twisted-pair cables or 16 Mbps using shielded twisted-pair cables. It is considered the most cost-effective architecture because of its consistent performance, effective management of data transmission over a network, reliability, accommodation of high workloads, and absence of collision.

Token ring is expensive in terms of both materials (i.e., cable, hub, and network cards) and maintenance (i.e., labor). It is more sophisticated to troubleshoot than Ethernet, but is more fault-tolerant and reliable. High-speed token ring (100 Mbps) also exists but is not widely deployed at this time.

## Fiber Distributed Data Interface Architecture

FDDI LAN is the most expensive networking architecture of the three discussed here. It uses a token-passing technology, runs at 100 Mbps (10 times as fast as Ethernet and about twice as fast as T-3), and can extend up to sixty miles in distance. FDDI is falling out of networking as a backbone technology because of its limited speed. ATM and high-speed Ethernet are the current favorites for backbones.

# NETWORK PROTOCOLS

One of the most commonly use network protocols is Transmission Control Protocol/Internet Protocol (TCP/IP ). TCP/IP is a suite of protocols that has become the standard for communication over the Internet. "TCP/IP is a routable protocol, and the IP part of TCP/IP provides the routing capability. In a routable protocol, all messages contain not only the address of the destination station, but [also] the address of a destination network. This allows TCP/IP messages to be sent to multiple networks within an organization or around the world" (TechWeb 2001). Most PC operating systems (e.g., Windows, Linux) have TCP/IP capabilities.

# WIRELESS LANS (WLANs)

A WLAN "is a flexible data communications system implemented as an extension to, or as an alternative for, a wired LAN. Using radio frequency (RF) technology, wireless LANs transmit and receive data over the air, minimizing the need for wired connections. Thus, wireless LANs combine data connectivity with user mobility" (Proxim, Inc. 2000). A WLAN requires two components: access points and adapters. Wireless access points are external transmitters and receivers, called transceivers, that use an RJ-45 or other connection to link to a wired network. Wireless adapters come in PC card formats for laptop computers or as internal ISA/PCI cards for desktop PCs. The leading companies that offer WLANs are

Lucent Technologies, Inc. (Orinoco, formerly WaveLAN), Nortel Networks (BayStack 660), Samsung (MagicLAN), Nokia (Nokia C110/C111), Cisco (Aironet 340), Zoom Telephonics (ZoomAir 4100), SMC Networks (EZConnect), and Apple Computers (Airport). These WLANs transmit data ranging from 1 Mbps to 11 Mbps (Hinde 2000). WLANs are now part of the IEEE standard 802.11b. This standard "defines wireless LANs that operate at 11 Mbps using a frequency in the 2.4 GHz range" (Comer 2001, 11). This standard covers two aspects: Frequency Hopping Spread-Spectrum (FHSS) and Direct-Sequence Spread-Spectrum (DSSS). Selected companies for wireless and other LANs are listed in Table 7.2.

Various technology options to choose from when designing a WLAN solution are described below.

## Table 7.2. Selected Networking Companies

| Name | Web Address* and Phone Number |
|------|-------------------------------|
| AT&T Network Systems | http://www.ipservices.att.com/products (800) 288-3199 |
| BreezeCOM | http://www.alvarion.com/HomPage.asp (760) 517-3100 |
| Cisco | http://www.cisco.com (800) 553-6387 |
| IBM Corporation | http://www.ibm.com (800) IBM 4 YOU |
| Lucent Technologies, Inc. | http://www.lucent.com (800) 238-1087 |
| Microdyne Corporation | http://www.microdyne.com (800) 792-6567 |
| Nortel Networks | http://www.nortelnetworks.com (800) 4-NORTEL |
| Proxim, Inc. | http://www.proxim.com (800) 229-1630 |
| Samsung | http://www.samsung.com (408) 544-5151 |
| Solectek Corporation | http://www.solectek.com (858) 450-1220 |
| Waters Network Systems | http://www.watersnet.com (763) 509-7425 |

* URLs last accessed October 29, 2001.

## Narrowband Technology

Narrowband transmits and receives data over a specific radio frequency. Users send and receive data over different radio channel frequencies, thus avoiding crosstalk between communication channels.

## Spread Spectrum Technology

Spread spectrum technology consumes more bandwidth than a narrowband radio frequency but provides a better signal that is easier to detect. There are two types of spread spectrum radio: FHSS and DSSS. FHSS uses a narrowband carrier, then hops from one frequency to another in a pattern known to both the transmitter and the receiver. It provides immunity to interference. DSSS sends data in redundant bits over a wide range of the spectrum. It is more susceptible to radio interference than FHSS but offers a higher data transfer rate than FSSS (11 Mbps vs. 2 Mbps, respectively) (Miles 1999).

Another type of WLAN is Infrared (IR), which uses the invisible part of light to carry data. It is usually limited to short distances because infrared cannot penetrate through opaque objects (Hinde 2000).

# SUMMARY

There are three main types of networks: LAN, MAN, and WAN. All these networks have three main components: cabling, topology, and protocol or architecture. The selection of a LAN cabling system (e.g., STP, UTP, coaxial, fiber optics), a topology (e.g., bus, star, ring), and protocol (e.g., Ethernet, token ring, FDDI) should be based on the media center's or library's existing and future applications, the data transmission speed desired, reliability, security, ease of installation and maintenance, and affordability. Each cabling system, topology, and protocol or architecture has advantages and disadvantages, which should be carefully examined in relation not only to the media center's or library's needs and requirements but also to the needs and requirements of the host institution.

Wireless network is another type that has become popular in the last few years. A wireless LAN (WLAN) does not use cables; rather, it requires two components: access points and adapters. Three main technology options are available for designing a WLAN: narrowband, spread spectrum, and infrared.

A LAN also requires a network operating system (NOS), which varies with the type of LAN in place (e.g., peer-to-peer, client/server). A network interface card (NIC) is also needed for coordinating the transmission and receipt of data over a LAN. NICs also vary with the LAN protocol used (e.g., token ring, Ethernet).

Qualified personnel should be available on site to diagnose and troubleshoot network problems so that user access is not hampered. To maintain the network's long-term reliability and to reduce the money and time spent on its maintenance, consider hiring certified personnel to design and install the cabling system, even though it is expensive.

A LAN is expensive to install and maintain. Therefore, it should be protected from unauthorized users by installing security software, such as firewalls. Measures should also be taken to ensure that the LAN components (e.g., wiring closet, servers) are located in safe places away from user access.

# REFERENCES

Black Box Network Services. 2000. *The cable catalog*. Lawrence, PA: Black Box. Network Services. Also available online at http://www.blackbox.com. (Accessed October 29, 2001).

Cisco. 2001. Available: http://www.cisco.com. (Accessed October 29, 2001).

Comer, Douglas E. 2001. *Computer networks and Internets with Internet applications*. 3d ed., Upper Saddle River, NJ: Prentice-Hall.

Hinde, Howard. 2000. No borders-no boundaries: Wireless LAN overview [Online]. Available: http://www.thedukeofurl.org/reviews/network/wirelesslan. (Accessed October 29, 2001).

Miles, J. B. 1999. Wireless LANS [Online]. Available: http://www.gcn.com/vol18_no28/guide/514-1.html. (Accessed on October 29, 2001).

Proxim, Inc. 2000. Selecting a wireless LAN technology [Online]. Available: http://www.proxim.com/products. (Accessed October 29, 2001).

Shelly, Gary B., et. al. 2000. *Discovering computers*. Cambridge, MA: Course Technology.

Stallings, William. 2001. *Business data communications*. 4th ed. Upper Saddle River, NJ: Prentice Hall.

TechWeb. 2001. Available: http://www.techweb.com. (Accessed October 29, 2001).

What is?.Com. 2001. Available: http://whatis.techtarget.com. (Accessed October 29, 2001).

## URLs of Companies Offering WLANs

Lucent Technologies, Inc. 2001. Available: http://www.lucent.com.

Nokia. 2001. Available: http://www.nokia.com/main.html.

Nortel Networks. 2001. Available: http://www.nortelnetworks.com/index.html.

Samsung. 2000. Available: http://www.samsung.com.

SMC Networks. 2000. Available: http://www.smc.com/smc/pages_html/homef.html.

Zoom Telephonics. 2001. Available: http://www.zoom.com.

# *Activity: Networking*

**Objective 1:** To explore a LAN's hardware and software requirements.
**Description:**

1. Select a media center or small library that has a LAN in place. Make an appointment with a person who is knowledgeable about the LAN (e.g., media specialist or information professional, technology specialist, technology coordinator, or other personnel). Take a brief tour of the facility where the LAN is located. Ask questions to learn the following about the LAN:

   Cabling system (e.g., coaxial, twisted-pair, fiber optics);

   Topology (e.g., star, bus, ring);

   Architecture (e.g., Ethernet, Fast Ethernet, token ring);

   Network operating system (NOS) (e.g., Novell Netware, Windows NT);

   Type of LAN (e.g., client/server, peer-to-peer);

   Number of workstations connected to the LAN;

   Workstations operating system (OS) (e.g., Windows, MAC);

   Number of servers used and for what purposes (e.g., mail server, Web server, database server);

   Number of hubs, routers, repeaters, as applicable, that support the LAN;

   Number of printers accessed over the LAN and the type of these printers (e.g., laser, inkjet);

   Location of servers; and

   Location of wiring closet.

2. Write a report describing the LAN components listed above. Include any other information you have obtained about the LAN.

# Chapter 8

---

## System Migration

---

System migration is the change from one automated system to another. This change can take two forms: upgrading an existing automated system using the same vendor or moving from one system to another using a new vendor. Regardless of the form of migration, however, every media center or library will eventually migrate to a new automated system at least once after its procurement of the original system. "What makes system migration different from your automation project is the necessity of migrating data from the original system to the new system. This is one of the most difficult aspects of migration" (Cervarich 1996).

### WHY MIGRATE?

Migration to a new system happens for many different reasons:

- The existing system does not support Internet or Web access (e.g., no TCP/IP).

- The existing system lacks modules that have become essential for the operation of the media center or library, and the vendor does not have plans for implementing these modules (e.g., interlibrary loan).

- The vendor of the existing system has no plans for supporting cutting edge technologies or new products that the media center or library may need in the near future.

- Vendor performance with the existing system is unsatisfactory.

- The existing system is DOS-based and the media center or library needs a Windows-based system.

- The existing system is inflexible and/or is not expandable. New applications (e.g., integrated acquisitions) cannot be supported.

**143**

- The school district is developing a wide area network (WAN) and therefore is requiring that media centers within the district have the same system or acquire a new system.

- The existing system is proprietary or locally developed and the media center or library would like to acquire an open, nonproprietary system.

- A new release of the existing system will be costly in terms of staff training, hardware replacement, and networking requirements.

# THE PROCESS OF MIGRATION

Most of the steps involved in selecting an automated system (see Chapter 4) apply to the migration process. This is especially true in terms of defining the needs of the media center or library and its clientele, evaluating existing systems, developing a request for proposal (RFP), evaluating vendors' responses to the RFP, and deciding on the system to procure. When defining needs this time around, it is important to assess the weaknesses and strengths of the existing system and unresolved system problems. You also should evaluate current hardware, network components and new products that are attractive to your media center or library but are not supported in the current system. In addition, evaluate the current vendor's performance and track records in terms of turnaround time for troubleshooting, improvements made since the procurement of the system, and future plans for system upgrade.

A sample RFP for procuring an automated system is provided in Chapter 4. Since you will be migrating to a new system, be sure to include additional functional specifications to the RFP that the current system does not have and that the new system under consideration should have.

In selecting a replacement vendor, consider

> The vendor's previous experience with successful data conversion or export of all types of records (circulation, bibliographic, vendor, etc.),

> The number of media centers or libraries for which the vendor has converted/exported data records, and

> The names of the automation software media centers or libraries a vendor has exported data records from and the names of the software a vendor has imported data records into.

The RFP must cover how the vendor will handle *circulation data, bibliographic data,* and other data supported in the current system. Questions to ask of the replacement vendor about *circulation data* include the following:

- How does the system handle current circulation transactions?

- How does the system handle overdues?

- How does the system handle holds?

- How does the system handle fines?

- How does the system handle fines that are pending?

- How does the system handle items with missing or lost status?

- How does the system handle reserve transactions?

- How does the system handle records created "on-the-fly?"

- What barcode symbologies does the system support?

It may be necessary to describe the type of problems the media center currently has with circulation data, as applicable, and/or current practices. For example, describe the barcode symbology supported in your current system and attach a sample of these barcodes to the RFP.

Questions to ask of the replacement vendor about *bibliographic data* include the following:

- What standards do you use for data records?

- How do bibliographic records relate to item records?

- How are links to bibliographic records, item records, and other interacting records established and broken?

- What fields exist in long bibliographic records?

- What fields exist in short bibliographic records?

- What fields are copied from a bibliographic record to a linked record?

- What data fields do you support in bibliographic records?

- What is the size of each data field in each type of record?

- How do you handle the export of nonstandard and customized MARC records?

- How do you handle MARC records imported from the Web that have missing data fields?

- How do you handle MARC records that contain errors in cataloging?

- To what extent do the MARC records you supply deviate from the standard MARC format (i.e., MARC 21)?

- How will the new system handle volume holdings?

- How will the new system handle multiple copy holdings?

- How will you handle authority records?

- What MARC field does your system support for local holdings?

Provide a description for some of the items listed above. For example, when asking about the MARC field for local holdings, mention whether your existing system supports field 852 or 900. Similarly, you may want to describe the most common cataloging errors, missing data fields, etc., that you have in current MARC records and attach a sample of these records to the RFP. Although the current system supports MARC standards, the MARC format used by different vendors may vary. In importing data from one system into another, make sure that each data element in a MARC record maps correctly.

## Database Cleanup

Be sure to clean up database records before replacing the existing system. Records for students or clients who are no longer affiliated with the host institution, for example, should be purged. Cleaning up the circulation records will save time and money. Following is a list of tasks that it would be helpful to do before replacing the existing system:

- Take an inventory of your collection and ensure that titles on the shelf are in the database and vice versa.

- Delete bibliographic records for which you have no holdings.

- Decide on what to do with records for missing or lost items. If you want to keep them, negotiate with the replacement vendor how the export of these items will be handled. The vendor will need detail about the codes you use for item status (e.g., lost, withdrawn, missing).

- Weed your collection and delete bibliographic records for withdrawn items.

- Decide whether you want to export temporary or "on-the-fly" records that you have created for paperbacks, vertical file items, etc. These records usually do not have bibliographic records. You may want to ask the replacement vendor to suggest strategies for handling these records.

- Identify bibliographic records that have data fields problem and correct them. These fields may include, but are not limited to, access points (main entry, title, added entries, subject headings, content notes); call numbers and call number prefixes; MARC tags, indicators, and subfield codes; misspellings; and abbreviations.

- Evaluate the currency of location codes, such as media center, classroom, computer laboratory, etc. If some codes have changed, make sure you provide detailed translation of these codes to the vendor so that the items with old codes can be mapped to the new codes.

- Evaluate the circulation database (transactions, fines, overdues, patron information). Purge records of patrons who are no longer affiliated with the host institution. Make sure that all overdues and fines are cleared. If not, discuss this matter with the replacement vendor to determine how to handle these records.

## Database Analysis

As discussed previously, one of the components of preparing the collection when you began the automation process was to analyze the shelflist (Chapter 5). Here you should analyze the bibliographic data in your cataloging database and the circulation data in your circulation database. If you have additional modules, you should analyze the data in each of these modules as well. Analysis of bibliographic data pertains to the practices used in creating and/or importing MARC records. You must be knowledgeable about the format of MARC standard supported in your current system and understand its designators (variable fields, fixed fields, tags, indicators, subfield codes, delimiters). Every vendor maintains a conversion checklist for data migration. Completing the checklist requires good knowledge of the collection and current practices. Follett Software Company (2001), for example, has a conversion checklist that includes a section on collection information. Completing this section will provide the vendor with a profile about current practices and future needs. This section has questions pertaining mainly to MARC tags and subfield codes used, including copy information, call number, location code, holdings code, circulation periods, ISBNs, LCCNs, author's name, volume information, item prices, vendor information, and barcodes. There are additional questions about the numerical range of barcodes, their length, and symbology used. The conversion of circulation data has its own set of questions.

It is important that you understand the nature of each data record and the database structure of the entire system. What is the relationship between a bibliographic record and an item record? You should understand the relationships of all records that interact during transactions. If you do not know your database structure, data relationships, and current practices, you will not be able to inform the vendor how certain data should be handled, and you will most likely encounter many problems in migrating to the new system. It will be useful to consult with colleagues at neighborhood libraries or over the Web who have been involved in the process of system migration and who use the same automated system to gain more knowledge about the structure of the database, among other things.

## Database Completion

If the media center or library has items that are not in the current system (i.e., not cataloged), you will have to decide how to handle these items. Will you catalog them before replacing the system or afterwards? Similarly, if the authority files for some items are not established, will you provide these authorities or wait until you migrate to the new system to do so? If the replacement vendor agrees to take care of all the odds and ends, make sure you dictate everything the replacement vendor promises to do in the contract. Remember that your institution does not have to pay for the new system in full upon installation. You may negotiate the terms and conditions of the contract and the payment schedule. Include your terms and conditions and payment schedule in the RFP. Following is an example of a payment schedule:

Successful installation of initial software (25 percent of total cost); successful installation of data migration and converted databases (40 percent of total cost); completion of training (15 percent of total cost); and successful completion of acceptance test (20 percent of total cost).

## Data Migration

You cannot rely solely on the vendor for the accuracy of data migration. In most cases, the media center or library staff are responsible for extracting data, for developing a plan to map records from the old system to the new one, and for testing the accuracy of data after the migration. Practitioners who have undergone the migration process suggest preparing data to test in the new system and developing a checklist of potential problem items to look at during the implementation process (Doering 2000). The vendor may ask you to test a data load. Have a sample of records on hand to test to determine whether all data look fine and are present. When working with patron information migration, for example, take a sample and verify that it was being done according to specifications outlined in the RFP and contract. If the sample is approved, then the processing of the entire patron database can be completed. When all patron data are loaded and mapped correctly into the new system, verify data for the second time and check coded fields to ensure that no code has been missed

(Broome 1997). If you are working with bibliographic records, determine whether records are formatted based on the latest MARC standard and that they are correctly formatted, that data are described based on the *Anglo-American Cataloging Rules* (*AACR2R*), and that all data are in the appropriate fields. Create problem records and test them in the new system to assure that the vendor is dealing with incorrect data correctly. Also provide a sample of records for test loading at each of the replacement vendors' sites (vendors that are finalists) before selecting a vendor and at contract time. Each vendor should identify records that do not load and determine the reason for failure to load. Sybrowsky (1991) lists additional tasks for data migration, including

> Mapping out where all the data contained in the sample will be put in the new database,
>
> Mapping out where all data needed by the new database will come from,
>
> Loading MARC records and mapping the data into both the bibliographic and item data files on the new system,
>
> Loading "static" patron data and verifying the data loaded, and
>
> Verifying that all data are loaded correctly into the new databases.

Provide a sample of barcodes supported in your current system to be tested for compatibility by the replacement vendor. The level of detail with which you document local media center or library practices and decisions in your current system will "affect the ease or lack of ease of later migration. Consistency in implementing these local decisions and practices affects how accurately you can migrate data" (Warwick 1994, 12). Try to run the old and the new system in tandem for a while until everything goes to your satisfaction. Do not discontinue product support of the current system too soon (Simpson 1999) and especially before completing the migration of all data from the old to the new system. Once everything is running smoothly, suspend the operation of the old system and begin using the new system fully. Back up the old system prior to switching to the new system.

Sample loading can also be part of the contract with the replacement vendor. "The contract should specify that the vendor will successfully load the data samples within a specified time frame and provide written notification to the library upon load completion" (Agnew and Lambert 1996, 6). The vendor should be given a reasonable time to correct data loading (e.g., thirty days). Data testing should include all types of records (bibliographic, patron, authority, circulation transactions, etc.).

When testing data, look for

> Long MARC records with 520 and 505 field tags;
>
> Bibliographic records for multivolume items;
>
> Bibliographic records for multiple copy items;
>
> Patron records (fines, overdues, address, status, etc.);
>
> Short MARC records, long and/or complex call numbers; and
>
> MARC records with attached item records (Doering 2000).

Migrating to a new system may also require redesigning existing facilities, upgrading the existing local area network's performance, and upgrading existing or purchasing new hardware and equipment. After the new system is implemented and tested for proper operation, staff and user training should be provided. System performance should be evaluated on a regular basis and problems should be relayed to the vendor.

# MIGRATION TIPS

Wilson (1994) offers the following tips for those considering system migration:

- Do not expect a smooth transition, because there will be problems.

- Check every detail of the RFP specifications and the replacement vendor's migration proposal.

- Have a detailed checklist for every aspect of system functionality currently in use (in the original system).

- Measure the checklist against the new system. Many aspects of the old system may not be supported in the new system.

- Avoid short-term "fixes" provided by the replacement vendor, especially if these fixes may give rise to further problems.

- Invest heavily in training.

- If system performance is not satisfactory, insist on performance audits on site.

# SUCCESSFUL MIGRATION

Successful system migration depends on many factors, including, but not limited to, the following:

> The experience of the replacement vendor,
> Your level of understanding of database structure and relationships between records that interact during transaction,
> Adequate planning and preparation for migration,
> The level of staff involvement,
> Effective communication among staff members,
> Effective communication with the vendor and other parties involved,
> User involvement,
> Data extraction for testing,
> The level of understanding of how both the old and new system handle and map data,
> Provision of sufficient time for data transfer,
> Thorough testing of the system after the migration,
> Specifications outlined in the RFP, and
> Contract negotiation.

# SUMMARY

System migration can be a very time-consuming activity. A good plan for carrying out the migration project is essential. Have a timeline for completing every aspect of the project. Know who your contact people are at the vendor's site. Document every communication with the vendor. Involve staff in the migration project because their experience and knowledge of automation can contribute positively to the migration project. Do your best to develop an RFP that contains every specification you must have in the new system. Review current literature on automation, preview automation software packages, and visit neighborhood libraries that have undergone migration using the same systems you have under consideration and those that have selected the same system you did. Gather information about their data migration, the problems they encountered, and the approach they took to solve these problems.

It is highly essential that you have a good understanding of the current database structure and the relationships between records that interact during transactions. In addition, be sure to document current practices and decisions so that you are able to communicate them to the replacement vendor. Testing sample data from different types of records (e.g., bibliographic records, item records, patron information) beforehand will give you an idea about what works and what fails. Good data mapping is one of the essential components of a successful migration.

Automation is a never-ending activity. After you migrate to a new system, you may have to change over to another system again in a few years.

# REFERENCES

Agnew, Grace, and Tomi Lambert. 1996. *Online system migration guide*. Chicago: Library and Information Technology Association.

Broome, Janet. 1997. The perfect migration. In *Planning and implementing successful system migrations*. Edited by Graeme Muirhead. London: Library Association, 182-87.

Cervarich, Catherine S. 1996. System migration: A bibliographic essay. In *Introducing and managing academic library automation projects*. Edited by John W. Head and Gerard B. McCabe. Westport, CT: Greenwood Press, 161-70.

Doering, William. 2000. Managing the transition to a new library catalog: Tips for smooth sailing. *Computers in Libraries* [Online]. Available: http://www.infotoday.com/cilmag/jul00/doering.htm. (Accessed October 29, 2001).

Follett Software Company. 2001. *Checklist for successful custom conversion of bibliographic data*. McHenry, IL: Follett Software Company.

Simpson, Carol. 1999. Migration, a moving experience. *Book Report* (May/June): 49-51.

Sybrowsky, Paul K. 1991. A vendor's perspective: Dynix on system migration. In *Library system migration: Changing automated systems in libraries and information centers*. Edited by Gary M. Pitkin. Westport, CT: Mechler, 124-33.

Warwick, Robert T. 1994. Moving to a new automated system: Some issues. *New Jersey Libraries* 27 (Spring): 11-14.

Wilson, Maurice. 1994. Talis at Nene: An experience in migration in a college library. *Program* 28 (July): 239-51.

# *Activity: System Migration*

**Objective**: To gain experience in various activities involved in system migration.

**Description**:

1. Select a media center or library that is undergoing migration from one automated system to another.

2. Contact the person in charge of the migration project and set an appointment for a visit to the media center or library and an interview with the project leader.

3. Give the name of the media center or library, the name of the project leader or staff member you interviewed, the phone number of the media center or library, and the day and time of the visit.

4. Name the automated system that the media center or library currently has and the new system it will be procuring.

5. Describe why the media center or library is changing over to a new system. Include the problems the current system has, if any; the track record of the vendor of the current system; and any other reasons for the migration.

6. Describe the process of migration the project leader and/or staff has/have undertaken.

7. List the concerns and/or issues that the project leader and/or staff need to handle during and after the migration.

8. Write a report and describe your experience with this activity.

# Chapter 9

## OPACs and the World Wide Web

The World Wide Web (Web) has revolutionized how people access, retrieve, and manage information. Regardless of the type and size of a library, maintaining a presence on the Web has become the "norm." Unlike any information retrieval system, the Web offers seamless access to information worldwide.

When the first edition of this book appeared in 1997, the Web was in its infancy. Most libraries had their collections available on Gopher, Telnet, or Hytelnet. Gopher was a menu-driven Internet application software that provided a hierarchical structure to its menus. Gopher allowed searching and navigating the Internet by making menu-based choices. Keyword searching was provided via indexes such as Veronica and Jughead.

Telnet is a client software for establishing communications between a local and a remote computer. It is one of the protocols of the Internet. Access to an OPAC is made possible by issuing a telnet command to the OPAC's address. To telnet to Lincoln High School OPAC in Oregon, for example, you type TELNET dynix1.pps.k12.or.us.

Hytelnet is a hypertext-based directory of telnet sites on the Internet. It was compiled in 1990 by Peter Scott but is no longer being maintained. Online catalogs available via Hytelnet can still be found at http://www.lights.com/hytelnet (Scott 1997). Today, access to OPACs is via the Web. To find Web-based OPACs worldwide, for example, point your browser to LibDex at http://www.libdex.com.

The Web is a hypertext-based multimedia information retrieval system that integrates text, images, video, and sound. To take full advantage of using the Web, a Web browser (e.g., Netscape) is needed. The Web offers a powerful, new way to make a media center or library's collection accessible. Having an OPAC available on the Web will provide expanded access to a media center or library's collection by integrating the collection with pertinent Web resources. It will also improve patrons' services by allowing them to place holds on needed items remotely, issue interlibrary loan requests for items not housed locally, and view an institution's events and activities, among other things.

# OPAC ON THE WEB

To make your OPAC accessible on the Web, you need to have a local area network (LAN) or a wide area network (WAN), Internet access with a dedicated Internet address (IP) and a leased telephone line, a connection to a Web server (hardware), an operating system, a Web server software, a Web browser, and Transmission Control Protocol/Internet Protocol (TCP/IP). It is also advisable to have a Z39.50 server to allow patrons around the world to search your collection using a Z39.50 client. The Z39.50 standard allows systems to execute, retrieve, and display information using a common interface, regardless of the hardware, software, platform, database structure, content, or format employed in a particular automated system. System requirements may vary from one automated system to another. Check with your system vendor about the system requirements needed to support publishing your collection on the Web.

The TCP/IP is one of the Internet protocols that facilitates communications among various computer networks, regardless of the operating systems, languages, and hardware employed. In simple terms, this protocol can be thought of in two portions: TCP can be thought of as a post office and IP as a home address.

OPACs on the Web are also referred to as Internet public access catalogs (IPACs) and Web public access catalogs (Web PACs).

## Access to OPACs on the Web

Many libraries' OPACs are available for searching on the Web. Web66 registry is the most comprehensive site for K–12 libraries around the world. It is found at http://web66. coled.umn.edu/schools.html. The site is maintained by Stephen E. Collins. After publishing your OPAC on the Web, you may want to add it to Web66 to make it accessible worldwide. To do so, contact Collins at schools@web66.coled.umn.edu.

LibWeb lists over 5,700 pages from different types of libraries in more than 100 countries and allows searching by keyword. It is available at http://sunsite.Berkeley.edu/ Libweb. The site is maintained by Thomas Dowling. If you wish to add your media center's or library's OPAC to the list, contact Dowling at tdownling@ohiolink.edu.

Individual OPACs can also be found under the name of a media center or library by searching Web search engines such as AlltheWeb (http://www.alltheweb.com) or meta-search engines such as Northern Light (http://www.northernlight.com). A phrase search may be the most precise method for finding the URL of a media center or library. A search for the Webb School located in Knoxville, Tennessee, for example, is entered in AlltheWeb as "Webb School." The quotation marks indicate to the search engine to locate documents that have these two words very close to each other, thus producing precise results. A phrase search is more accurate than a Boolean search. Once you locate a school's Web site, click on the link that directs you to the media center or library.

## Searching OPACs with the Z39.50 Standard

Automated systems vary with regard to hardware, operating systems and platforms, and applications software used. Because of these variations, the search commands, features, and screen displays for various OPACs differ from one to another. "Z39.50 is a national standard defining a protocol for computer-to-computer information retrieval. Z39.50 makes it possible for a user in one system to search and retrieve information from other computer systems (that have also implemented Z39.50) without knowing the search syntax that is used by those other systems. Z39.50 is an American National Standard that was originally approved by the National Information Standards Organization (NISO) in 1988" (Library of Congress 2001).

The Library of Congress has a site dedicated to Z39.50, including OPACs. To access this site, point your browser to http://lcweb.loc.gov/z3950/gateway.html. Most vendors, if not all, have implemented this standard in their automated systems.

The implementation of the Z39.50 standard, which standardized the appearance and command functions of OPACs over the Web, has made it possible for users to search various OPACs using one common interface and command language, thus making OPACs from around the world easier to search.

## Benefits of OPACs on the Web

OPACs on the Web offer a wide array of benefits as they open new avenues for global information access and increased accessibility to library collections. Users can search OPACs from any remote location and are no longer confined to the local boundaries of specific media centers or libraries. Users can access OPACs from homes, offices, or elsewhere and around the clock. They can identify the materials they need, determine whether the materials are available in their local libraries, and issue interlibrary loan (ILL) requests for borrowing materials not available locally. Appropriate ILL forms can be generated and completed online through a library's home page and mailed directly to the lending library, provided such features are implemented.

OPACs on the Web serve as gateways to the vast amount of information available. Access to libraries' union catalogs (a collection of districtwide or statewide online catalogs) encourages resource sharing among libraries, thus reducing the cost of collection development. Online OPACs also provide media specialists and information professionals with new means for evaluating their library collections; they can compare their collections to those of other media centers or libraries. Access to millions of bibliographic MARC records is available. When searching for information in a Z39.50 OPAC, for example, one can view the MARC record of the item found and save it for later import into one's automation database. If import is not possible, one can still use the cataloging information to input into the database. This free service reduces the time and cost of cataloging resources. The Library of Congress provides full access to its OPAC (http://catalog.loc.gov), which contains 12 million records of various media. This OPAC has an alternative interface in Z39.50 that can be found at the Library of Congress Z39.50 Gateway (http://lcweb.loc.gov/z3950). MARC records can be displayed and saved on one's computer hard disk or other peripherals.

In the chaotic world of the Web, OPACs offer a well-structured and organized sub-world in which information is classified, indexed, and retrieved according to established standards. This is important because even experienced searchers find it difficult to locate specific information on the Web. As media centers and other libraries become hubs of information, they will need to shift their focus from local information access to global information access. OPACs on the Web are ideal information tools that not only provide users with access to earthly information but also empower them with online searching skills that are needed to unravel this world of information.

## Issues in Accessing OPACs on the Web

Enhancing a media center's or library's collection by adding Web resources, although beneficial, may subject the media center or library to budget cuts. This may happen if administrators lack adequate understanding of the nature of Web resources; that is, volatility. Therefore, it is important that media specialists or information professionals describe the nature of these resources and the issues involved in using them to their administrators. One of these issues is reliability. To ensure that Web resources that are linked to existing collections and that appear in the OPAC are "alive and well," media specialists or information professionals must examine these resources on a regular basis. This chore is time-consuming. An alternative is to subscribe to an automation vendor's Web service that automatically links the Web from a local OPAC by integrating MARC tag field 856 that is reserved to URLs. This type of service does not require any local update of Web sites because it is provided at the vendor's location. Any time a user clicks on a site from the OPAC, the site goes to the vendor's Web server for authentication and verification before it is directly linked to the Web. Subscribing to such a service will ensure that all Web sites linked to the OPAC are available.

Access to free MARC records on the Web raises the issue of accuracy and reliability. Many records contain errors in cataloging and in using MARC standards. Therefore, if you use any MARC records, especially those that are not from the Library of Congress, clean them up before or after you input them into your cataloging database. Fee-based MARC records available via the Web, such as EZCat Pro (http:// www.booksys.com), are more reliable than those available in the public domain, such as SUNLINK (http://www.sunlink.ucf.edu).

# SUMMARY

The presence of OPACs on the Web has become the "norm." All vendors will eventually provide a software program that allows media centers and libraries to publish their collections on the Web. Publishing your OPAC on the Web will expand your collection, enhance your services to patrons, and increase the visibility of the media center or library, not only locally but also worldwide.

# REFERENCES

Library of Congress. 2001. Z39.50 Gateway to Library Catalogs. Available: http://lcweb.loc.gov/z3950/gateway.html. (Accessed October 28, 2001).

Scott, Peter. 1997. Hytelnet home page. Available: http://www.usask.ca/~scottp. (Accessed on October 28, 2001).

# Activity: Access to Z39.50 OPACs

**Objective 1:** To gain experience in searching Z39.50 OPACs on the Web.

**Description:** Connect to the Library of Congress Z39.50 Gateway at http://lcweb. loc.gov/z3950/gateway.html.

1.  Select any OPAC to search.

2.  Perform an author, title, subject, and keyword search in the OPAC.

3.  View the search record for the item you looked for.

4.  View the MARC record for the item you looked for.

5.  Print the MARC record you have located.

**Objective 2:** To compare MARC records found in a Z39.50 OPAC to MARC records found in the SUNLINK database.

**Description 1:** Connect to SUNLINK at http://www.sunlink.ucf.edu.

1.  Select one OPAC or search the entire database.

2.  Perform an author, title, subject, and keyword search in the OPAC.

3.  View the search record for the item you looked for.

4.  View the MARC record for the item you looked for.

5.  Print the MARC record you have located.

**Description 2:** Compare the quality of MARC records found in both databases. Write a report describing your experience with this activity. Attach copies of the MARC records you printed.

# Chapter 10

---

## Future OPACs

---

Advancement in information technology has had a marked impact on library automation in general and on OPACs in particular. The popularity the Web has gained has influenced the type of products that vendors are to develop and the type of services that libraries are to deliver to patrons (the term *libraries* is used here for all types of libraries, including media centers). As the very nature of information access and delivery changes, so does the role of libraries, from ownership of information to access to information, and from acquiring and housing technologies to pathfinders of information. This chapter describes recent developments in library automation and discusses the most important trends and issues. The term *information professionals* includes both librarians and media specialists.

### RECENT DEVELOPMENTS IN LIBRARY AUTOMATION

First-generation OPACs were replicas of the traditional card catalog that provided searching by author, title, and subject. The second-generation OPACs incorporated enhanced and expanded features that included searching by author, title, subject, and keyword; Boolean operators; and proximity operators and allowed limiting search results to specific fields, such as publication date, type of material, and events. The third-generation OPACs have taken advantage of the client/server computing architecture and the Z39.50 standard. In fact, the client/server architecture has become the focal point of attention in library automation, as it has in the computing industry. The Windows NT operating system has made it possible for automation vendors to implement the client/server architecture and introduce it to small and medium-sized libraries that cannot otherwise afford a Unix-based client/server architecture. "The competitive relationship of Unix and Windows NT has been widely but inconclusively debated in business periodicals and computer magazines" (Saffady 2000, 27). For additional information about this architecture, see Chapter 3.

159

The Z39.50 standard permits users to access multiple information systems from their local computers, independent of the databases, search engines, hardware platform, application software, or servers used. The Z39.50 standard employs a client/server technology. A user with a Z39.50-compliant client can search any Z39.50 servers where online catalogs, bibliographic databases, reference databases, or CD-ROM databases reside, using the familiar interface and operating procedures of the client.

Integrated online catalogs have supported the local mounting of reference databases. These databases can be acquired from either database publishers or automation vendors for a fee. Sagebrush Technologies, for example, supplies reference databases suitable for school libraries that can be mounted on the OPAC and searched using the OPAC syntax. This service expands the functionality of the OPAC and saves patrons time and effort that they may otherwise spend on learning the syntax of every database available.

Since 1998, there has been increased demand for the Graphical User Interface (GUI) and Web-based products. Most libraries have already migrated from character-based systems (DOS) to Windows- and Web-based systems. In a survey of automation vendors' opinions about the future of character-based systems, vendors' responses ranged from "short-lived" to "no future" (Barry, Bilal, and Penniman 1998). Vendors will soon cease to enhance or support these products. This trend will force libraries to shift to Windows-based interfaces even when they are unprepared for the migration. Because they are GUI-based, Windows-based systems offer pull-down menus, pop-up windows, multi-tasking, "point and click" operations using a mouse, and icons that represent functions, thereby simplifying functions and minimizing use of command language. However, GUI-systems will require upgrading of computer hardware. The cost of such an upgrade may be costly, especially to small libraries that are still operating their automation software on low-end computers. Libraries may need to assess their needs and phase in their migration by running DOS and GUI interfaces in tandem until a full transition is made.

The exponential use of the Web worldwide has made Web-based OPACs largely accepted by users. "The Web has represented a true revolution regarding information access and retrieval. For the first time in history, users in any part of the world can access all types of information independent of its physical storage or of the computer system used" (Ortiz-Repiso 1999, 3). The Web has facilitated the implementation of OPACs into this medium. All vendors offer a Web interface for their automated systems. Web-based OPACs permit users to access information from any local or remote location where an Internet connection is provided, thereby giving them increased and convenient access to the OPAC. User familiarity with Web browsers (e.g., Netscape, Internet Explorer) provides a common interface that may simplify training in using functions, such as e-mailing records, saving records, and printing records. However, using the Web will require adding a new dimension to user instruction programs or information literacy skills, because users will need to master the rules and operations of two interfaces, the OPAC and the Web browser it embraces. Training in effective and efficient Web navigation is central to using the Web successfully.

Another major development has been the Dublin Core Metadata Element Set, a standard for cataloging Internet resources. Most vendors have implemented this standard in their automation software, including vendors of microcomputer-based systems such as Follett Software Company and Sagebrush Technologies. Cataloging Internet resources and adding them to the OPAC expands access to a library's collection and increases the functionality of the OPAC. Once cataloged, each Internet resource will be linked to its pertinent MARC record in tag 856. This tag is reserved for a record's URL and is a repeatable field, meaning that more than one URL can be added to a MARC record. The main issue in adding Internet resources to the OPAC is updating them regularly to ensure their presence. The volatility of Internet resources makes updating a daunting task for information professionals. Many vendors have responded to this issue by introducing software that adds appropriate Internet resources to a bibliographic database. Follett's WebPath Express (formerly 856 Express), for example, is a subscription service that integrates 856 tags to a library's database. As of March 2001, it included more than 5,000 links that are evaluated for content and appropriateness and currency. As described by the vendor, this service allows staff to view and evaluate subscription usage and to identify heavily accessed subject areas to aid in collection development. One does not expect to find an obsolete link because the editors update the links on a daily basis (see Follett site at http://www.fsc.follett.com/products). Although this service is convenient and saves time in adding and updating URLs to the OPAC, it may be costly for many small libraries that operate on a small budget. The cost of the service is expected to decrease, however, as similar products become widely available in the near future. At the time of writing, a WebPath Express annual subscription was $995.

In 1999, many vendors added new cutting-edge technologies to their automation software. They developed cross-platform products, expanded the application of GUI across different modules of software, developed intranet/web applications, implemented digital collections, continued support for the Electronic Data Interface (EDI) for online acquisitions, and introduced next-generation telephone notification service. In addition, some vendors provided support for sophisticated programming and coding languages, such as Java and eXtensible Markup Language (XML) (Bilal, Barry, and Penniman 1999). The XML standard creates bibliographic records once and publishes them in different formats. Bibliographic records can be viewed by Web browsers, search engines, and library systems without further conversions. In addition, "bibliographic records can be interchanged between XML and MARC without data loss" (Ortiz-Repiso 1999, 3).

Multiple language interfaces using the Unicode standard became of interest to many vendors who were entering the international automation marketplace. Media centers and small libraries may not benefit from these cutting-edge technologies immediately because they are expensive to implement.

There was a new development in outsourcing systems support and services in 2000. Libraries that were experiencing difficulties with financial resources started outsourcing their software and hardware to automation vendors. This new outsourcing model is called access service provider (ASP). In this model, vendors are the service providers who maintain the software and hardware at a centralized location via the Web. "As network bandwidth improves, we will begin to see libraries that have their entire bibliographic database residing at a vendor's site and all processing and transactions done over the network" (Barry 2000, 2). Data Research Associates (DRA), the vendor of DRA Classic, Inlex/3000, MultiLIS, and Taos automation software; and Epixtech, formerly Ameritech Library Services (ALS), have been the leaders in exploring this model for academic libraries. Fortunately, CASPR Library Systems, Inc., has taken a leadership role in exploring this model for the school library marketplace. For small and medium-sized, including school, libraries this model can be very attractive (Barry 2000). As the cost of this service decreases, it will save librarians time and money in managing their software and hardware. Librarians who are exploring this model should assess their library needs vis-à-vis the cost and quality of the ASP service. In addition, they should determine how much control the ASP will have over their software and hardware.

The School Interoperability Framework (SIF) is a new trend for school libraries. SIF is "a technical blueprint for K-12 software that will enable diverse applications to interact and share data efficiently, reliably and securely, regardless of platform. Schools will be able to share student demographics, attendance information, library information, and grades" (Follett Software Company 2001, 1). SIF can eliminate redundant, tedious paperwork by enabling staff to share student information across the network rather than entering this information into each individual database (e.g., circulation database, student information database).

As patrons' needs have become a top priority for many vendors, companies such as The Library Corporation (TLC) are exploring ways for providing easy access to a world of information in a simple yet sophisticated manner. The sophisticated OPAC, as Gary Kirk, director of marketing for TLC system, claims, will aggregate full-text content, images, and other useful information in a meaningful and organized manner, all delivered from a graphical, personalized library Web portal. "YouSeeMore," is the concept of OPAC of the future, he asserts. This OPAC will display book covers, table of contents, first chapters, and reviews and will have the ability to purchase or borrow items. It will provide single search access to all the full-text information databases that the library offers and deliver that information with relevancy. The OPAC of the future will permit patrons to personalize their own library Web pages to obtain information, such as items checked out, due dates, and items on holds, as well as recommendations for new selections based on patrons' preferences or profiles (Kirk 2001).

Use of the Web offers many advantages to patrons and frees libraries from developing, maintaining, and distributing a proprietary software package that patrons will need to search the OPAC and retrieve information from it (Yee and Shatford 1998). However, the Web interface is "stateless," meaning that libraries do not own it and have no control over its access. In addition, this interface requires that users have powerful computers to run the Web browsing software. Patrons who have low-end computers will not benefit from using this technology.

The Web has not solved many of the underlying problems that patrons have experienced in using second-generation OPACs. Indeed, Web-based OPACs are founded on traditional cataloging practices, such as the concept of main and added entries, as well as the use of rigid classification systems and standardized subject heading lists that are far removed for the world of the users. OPAC interfaces have been developed from a professional perspective, a perspective that does not always take into consideration the end user. For users, the presence of technical vocabulary and the continued use of concepts far removed from their world make information access and retrieval difficult (Ortiz-Repiso 1999).

Research studies have shown that users experience problems in using second-generation OPACs. These problems pertain mainly to formulating search strategies, selecting appropriate terminology, using Boolean logic correctly, and managing information overload (Berger and Moore 1996; Borgman 1996; Borgman et. al. 1995; Solomon 1993; Larson 1992; Hunter 1991; Chen 1991; Edmonds, Moore, and Balcom 1990; Blazek and Bilal 1988; Borgman 1986; Markey 1986; Bates 1986). Studies of Web-based OPACs have recently appeared in academic libraries (Cooper 2001). As of March 2001, the library and information science literature did not have any evidence of such research undertaken in school libraries. Definitely, user studies of Web-based OPACs, especially in school libraries, are highly recommended. We must develop a good understanding of how users in K–12 environments seek information in Web-based OPACs. Such endeavors will help us make recommendations for system design improvements and will give us a framework for developing effective information literacy skills programs in using an OPAC.

The OPAC of the future should be user-centered not only in its interface design but also in the structure of its bibliographic database. The underlying structure (i.e., the MARC format) should not be the only format for encoding data. Other types of formats that are based on XML, for example, should be explored to facilitate the creation of "true hypertext databases" that are suitable for the Web environment (Ortiz-Repiso 1999). In addition, a user-centered OPAC should

Allow searching by natural language;

Provide online assistance that is context-driven and readily available;

Give relevance ranking of retrieved results;

Have meaningful icons that are well-labeled;

Model user information-seeking behaviors;

Integrate an online wizard that appears immediately as errors are committed or problems are encountered;

Incorporate a front-end intelligent interface or agent that guides users during the search and retrieval process; and

Integrate spell-checking techniques, especially in OPACs designed for children.

# ROLE OF INFORMATION PROFESSIONALS

Information professionals are constantly in direct contact with their users, whether in person or remotely. They serve as trainers, consultants, and information managers. These professionals should assume a leadership role in studying user information-seeking behavior to unravel problems that can be remedied through training and identify problems that should be addressed by system designers.

In addition, information professionals must add the use of Web-based OPACs to their existing user instruction or information literacy programs. In accessing a Web-based OPAC, users will operate in two spaces, the OPAC's space and the Web browser's space. Navigating in Web space can be difficult if users are not equipped with adequate skills to use a Web browser. Studies of children's use of the Web reveal that children were minimally successful in locating information, and that they were naïve in navigating Web space (Bilal 1998; 2000; 2001; Large and Beheshti 2000). Effective use of the Web is vital to using a Web-based OPAC.

Information professionals must shift from the traditional mode of thinking, organizing, and retrieving information to innovative approaches in delivering information services. There is no doubt that advancement in information technology will influence the type of services a library should provide to its users. Information professionals should revisit their library missions and evaluate their roles in serving the "patron of the future."

# REFERENCES

Barry, Jeff. 2000. Automated system marketplace 2000: Delivering the personalized library. *Library Journal* 125 (April 1): 49-60.

Barry, Jeff, Dania Bilal, and W. David Penniman. 1998. Automated system marketplace 98: The competitive struggle. *Library Journal* (April 1): 43-52.

Bates, M. 1986. Subject access in online catalogs: A design model. *Journal of the American Society for Information Science* 37 (6): 357-76.

Berger, Michael George, and Mary Jean Moore. 1996. The user meets the MELVYL system. *DLA Bulletin* 16 (1): 13-21.

Bilal, Dania. 1998. Children's search processes in using World Wide Web search engines: An exploratory study. In *Proceedings of the 61st ASIS Annual Meeting, 35, October 24-29, 1998, Pittsburgh*. Medford, NJ: Information Today, 45-53.

_____. 2000. Use of the Yahooligans! Web search engine. II. Cognitive and physical behaviors on research-based search tasks. *Journal of the American Society for Information Science* 52 (2): 118-36.

_____. 2001. Use of the Yahooligans! Web search engine. I. Cognitive, physical and affective behaviors on fact-based search tasks. *Journal of the American Society for Information Science* 51 (7): 646-65.

Bilal, Dania, Jeff Barry, and W. David Penniman. 1999. Automated system marketplace 98: A balancing act. *Library Journal* (April 1): 45-54.

Blazek, R., and Dania Bilal. 1988. Problems with OPAC: A case study of an academic library. *RQ* 28 (2): 169-78.

Borgman, C. L. 1996. Why are online catalogs still hard to use? *Journal of the American Society for Information Science* 47 (7): 493-503.

Borgman, Christine L. 1986. Why are online catalogs hard to use? Lessons learned from information retrieval studies. *Journal of the American Society for Information Science* 37 (6): 384-400.

Borgman, Christine L., et. al. 1995. Children's searching behavior on browsing and keyword searching online catalogs: The Science Library Catalog project. *Journal of the American Society for Information Science* 46 (9): 663-684.

Chen, Shu-Hsien. 1991. A study of online catalog searching behavior of high school students. Ed. D. Diss., University of Georgia.

Cooper, Michael D. 2001. Usage patterns of a Web-based catalog. *Journal of the American Society for Information Science and Technology* 52 (2): 137-48.

Edmonds, Leslie, Paula Moore, and Kathleen M. Balcom. 1990. The effectiveness of an online catalog. *School Library Journal* 36 (October): 28-32.

Hunter, Rhonda N. 1991. Successes and failures of patrons searching the online catalog at a large academic library: A transaction log analysis. *RQ* 30 (3): 395-402.

Kirk, Gary W. 2001. [Vice President, The Library Corporation]. E-mail communication with author, April 1.

Large, A., and Jamshid Beheshti. 2000. The Web as a classroom resource: Reactions from the users. *Journal of the American Society for Information Science & Technology* 51 (12): 1069-80.

Larson, R. R. 1992. Evaluation of advanced retrieval techniques in an experimental online catalog. *Journal of the American Society for Information Science* 43 (1): 34-53.

Markey, Karen, 1986. Users and the online catalog: Subject access problems. In *The impact of online catalogs*. Edited by J. R. Matthews. New York: Neal-Schuman, 35-70.

Ortiz-Repiso, Virginia. 1999. Web-based OPACs: Between tradition and innovation. *Information Technology and Libraries* 18 (2): 68-77.

Saffady, William. 2000. The status of library automation at 2000. *Library Technology Reports* 36 (1): 3-70.

Solomon, Paul. 1993. Children's information retrieval behavior: A case analysis of a OPAC. *Journal of the American Society for Information Science* 44 (5): 245-64.

Yee, Martha M., and Sara Lyne Shatford. 1998. *Improving online public access catalogs.* Chicago: American Library Association.

# Bibliography

AECT & AASL. 1998. *Information power: Building partnerships for learning*. Chicago: American Library Association.

Agnew, Grace, and Tomi Lambert. 1996. *Online system migration guide*. Chicago: Library and Information Technology Association.

Barry, Jeff. 2000. Automated system marketplace 2000: Delivering the personalized library. Library Journal 125 (April 1): 49-60.

———. 2001. Automated system marketplace 2001: Closing in on Content. *Library Journal* 126 (April 1): 46-52.

Barry, Jeff, Dania Bilal, and W. David Penniman. 1998. Automated system marketplace 98: the competitive struggle. *Library Journal* (April 1): 43-52.

Beiser, Karl. 1999a. Integrated library system software for smaller libraries. Part 1. Special, academic and public libraries. *Library Technology Reports* 35 (2): 119-262.

———. 1999b. Integrated library system software for smaller libraries. Part 2. School, academic, and public libraries. *Library Technology Reports* 35 (4): 365-95.

Bilal, Dania. 1998. Children's search processes in using World Wide Web search engines: An exploratory study. *Proceedings of the 61st ASIS Annual Meeting, 35, October 24-29, Pittsburgh*. Medford, NJ: Information Today, 45-53.

———. 2000. Children's use of the Yahooligans! Web search engine. II. Cognitive and physical behaviors on Research tasks. *Journal of the American Society for Information Science* 52 (2): 118-36.

———. 2001. Children's use of the Yahooligans! Web search engine. I. Cognitive, physical, and affective behaviors on fact-based tasks. *Journal of the American Society for Information Science* 51 (7): 646-65.

Bilal, Dania, Jeff Barry, and W. David Penniman. 1999. Automated system marketplace 98: A balancing act. *Library Journal* (April 1): 45-54.

Blodgett, Teresa, and Judi Repman. 1995. The electronic school library resource center: Facilities planning for the new information technologies. *Emergency Librarian* 22 (January/February.): 26-30.

Borgman, Christine L. 1999. What are digital libraries? Competing visions. *Information Processing & Management* 35 (May): 227-43.

Boss, Richard. 1997. *The library administrator's automation handbook*. Medford, NJ: Information Today.

———. 1998. Model technology plans for libraries. *Library Technology Reports* 34 (1): 9-109.

Broome, Janet. 1997. The perfect migration. In: *Planning and implementing successful system migrations*. Edited by Graeme Muirhead. London: Library Association Publishing, 182-87.

Buckland, Michael. 1992. *Redesigning library services: A Manifesto*. Chicago: American Library Association.

CASPR Library Systems. 2001. LibraryCom. Available: http://www.librarycom.com/\lc.exe/ Freemarc. (Accessed October 29, 2001).

Cervarich, Catherine S. 1996. System migration: A bibliographic essay. In *Introducing and managing academic library automation projects*. Edited by John W. Head and Gerard B. McCabe. Westport, CT: Greenwood Press, 161-70.

Comer, Douglas E. 2001. *Computer networks and Internets with Internet applications*. 3d ed. Upper Saddle River, NJ: Prentice-Hall.

Cooper, Michael D. 1996. *Design of library automation systems: File structures, data structures, and tools*. New York: John Wiley.

Crawford, Walt. 1989. *MARC for library use*. Boston: G. K. Hall.

Day, Teresa Thurman, Bruce Flanders, and Gregory Zuck. (Eds.) 1994. *Automation for school libraries*: *How to do it from those who have done it*. Chicago: American Library Association.

Doering, William. 2000. Managing the transition to a new library catalog: Tips for smooth sailing. *Computers in Libraries* [Online]. http://www.infotoday.com/cilmag/jul00/ doering.htm. (Accessed October 22, 2001).

Eisenberg, Michael. B., and Robert E. Berkowitz. 1990. *Information Problem-Solving*: *The Big6™ Skills Approach to Library & Information Skills Instruction*. Norwood, CT: Ablex Publishing.

Erikson, Rolf, and Carolyn Markuson. 2001. *Designing a school library media center for the future*. Chicago: American Library Association.

Everhart, Nancy. 1998. *Evaluating the school library media center*. Englewood, CO: Libraries Unlimited.

Furrie, Betty. 2000. *Understanding MARC bibliographic: Machine-Readable Cataloging*. Washington, DC: Library of Congress.

Gorman, Michael. 1989. *The concise AACR2R: 1988 revision*. Chicago: American Library Association.

Gorman, Michael, and Paul Winkler. 1988. *Anglo-American cataloguing rules, second revised rdition*. Chicago: American Library Association.

Hallmark, Julie, and Rebecca Garcia C. 1996. Training for automated systems in libraries: Views of library administrators and vendors. *Information Technology and Libraries* 15 (September): 151-63.

Horton, William. 2000. *Designing Web-based training*: *How to teach anyone anything anywhere anytime*. New York: John Wiley.

Kuhlthau, Carol C. 1993. *Seeking meaning*: *A process approach to library and information services*. Norwood, CT: Ablex.

Lankford, Mary D. 1994. Design for change: How to plan the school library you really need. *School Library Journal* 40 (February): 20-24.

Librarians Information Online Network (LION). 2000. Automation for School Librarians. Available: http://www.libertynet.org/lion/auto.html. (Accessed October 29, 2001).

The Library Corporation. 2000. ITS.MARC. Available: http://www.itsmarc.com. (Accessed October 29, 2001).

The Library of Congress. 2000a. MARC Record Services. Available: http://lcweb.loc.gov/marc/marcrecsvrs.html. (Accessed October 29, 2001).

———. 2000b. MARC Records, Systems, and Tools. Available: http://lcweb.loc.gov/marc. (Accessed October 29, 2001).

———. 2000c. Select MARC Retrospective Conversion Services. Available: http://lcweb.loc.gov/cds/selmarl.html. (Accessed October 29, 2001).

Manczuk, Suzanne, and R. J. Pasco. 1994. Planning for technology: A newcomer's guide. *Journal of Youth Services in Libraries* 7 (Winter): 199-206.

Mather, Becky R. 1997. *Creating a local area network in the school library media center.* Westport, CT: Greenwood Publishing.

Meghabghab, Dania Bilal. 1997. *Automating media centers and small libraries: A microcomputer-based approach.* Englewood, CO: Libraries Unlimited.

Minkel, Wlater, and Roxanne Hsu Feldman. 1999. *Delivering Web services to young people.* Chicago: American Library Association.

Morris, Anne, and Hilary Dyer. 1998. *Human aspects of library automation.* 2d ed. Brookfield, VT: Gower.

Ogg, Harold C. 1997. *Introduction to the use of computers in libraries.* Medford, NJ: Learned Information.

Ortiz-Repiso, Virginia. 1999. Web-based OPACs: Between tradition and innovation. *Information Technology and Libraries* 18 (2): 68-77.

Ralston, Anthony, Edwin D. Reilly, and David Hemmendinger (Eds.). 2000. *Encyclopedia of computer science.* London: Nature Publishing.

Saffady, William. 1999. *Introduction to computers for librarians.* Chicago: American Library Association.

———. 2000. The status of library automation at 2000. *Library Technology Reports* 36 (1): 3-70.

Shelly, Gary B., et. al. 2000. *Discovering computers.* Cambridge, MA: Course Technology.

Simpson, Carol. 1999. Migration, a moving experience. *Book Report* (May/June): 49-51.

Stallings, William. 2001. *Business data communications.* 4th ed. Upper Saddle River, NJ: Prentice Hall.

SUNLINK. 2000. Available: http://www.sunlink.ucf.edu. (Accessed October 29, 2001).

Swan, James. 1996a. *Automating small libraries.* Fort Atkinson. WI: Highsmith Press.

———. 1996b. Automating small libraries. *Rural Libraries* 16 (1): 7-22.

TLC. 2000. Available: http://www.auto-graphics.com/cgiojw/redir?txlc. (Accessed October 29, 2001).

Warwick, Robert T. 1994. Moving to a new automated system: Some issues. *New Jersey Libraries* 27 (Spring): 11-14.

White, Ron. 2002. *How computers work*. Indianapolis, IN: Que.

Wolfgram, Linda M. 1996. The effects of automation on school library media centers. *Journal of Youth Services in Libraries* 9 (Summer): 387-94.

Wright, Keith C. 1995. *Computer-related technologies on library operations*. Brookfield, VT: Gower.

Yee, Martha M., and Sara Lyne Shatford. 1998. *Improving online public access catalogs*. Chicago: American Library Association.

# Glossary

***AACR2R:*** *Anglo-American Cataloguing Rules, Second Revised Edition* (1988). A bibliographic standard based on a set of rules used to describe various types of library materials.

**ADSL:** *See* Asymmetric Digital Subscriber Line.

**Access service provider (ASP):** An emerging outsourcing model in which vendors are the service providers for libraries and maintain the software and hardware at a centralized location via the Web.

***Alliance Plus:*** A CD-ROM database of MARC records developed by Follett Software Company. It is mainly used for retrospective conversion.

**ASP:** *See* Access service provider.

**Asymmetric Digital Subscriber Line (ADSL):** A digital line that receives data ranging from 1.54 Mbps to 8.45 Mbps (downstream) and sends data ranging from 128 Kbps to 640 Kbps (upstream).

**ATM:** *See* Asynchronous Transfer Mode.

**Asynchronous Transfer Mode (ATM):** A service offered by Local Exchange Carriers (e.g., Bell South, Ameritech) and by the Interexchange Carriers (e.g., AT&T, MCI). It can be used over T-1 and T-3 lines. ATM transmits voice, data, video, and multimedia over a single line at high speeds (622 Mbps or higher). It is used in telephone networks, the Internet, or networks with high traffic.

**Authority control:** The process of grouping variant forms of a heading under one single heading for the purpose of maintaining consistency Authority control applies to personal author names, corporate bodies, subject headings, and series.

**Barcode:** A set of numbers represented by a pattern of bars that can be recognized by automation software. Barcodes are assigned to an item or patron. A barcode can be entered electronically using a hardware device (i.e., a barcode scanner) or manually by typing the numbers into an automated system.

**Barcode scanner:** A hardware device that is used to scan, read, and/or enter a barcode number into an automated system.

**Baseband:** A telecommunication system in which information is carried in digital form on a single signal channel on a transmission medium.

**Basic Rate Interface (BRI):** One of the level of services provided by an ISDN line supplier. It consists of two 64 kbps B-channels and one 16 Kbps D-channel, totaling 128kbps. It is used for homes and offices.

***Bibliofile:*** A CD-ROM database of MARC records developed by the Library Corporation. It is mainly used for retrospective conversion.

**Bibliographic database:** A collection of cataloging records in MARC 21 format.

**Bit:** The smallest unit of data in a computer. A bit has a single binary value, either 0 or 1.

**Boolean logic:** Logic based on Boolean algebra. It was developed by the logician George Boole. The main functions used in information retrieval are the operators *and* to narrow search results, *or* to expand search results, and *not* to narrow search results by eliminating unwanted terms. *See also* Nesting.

**BRI:** *See* Basic Rate Interface.

**Bridge:** A hardware device that converts data between networks that have different architecture and that have similar datalink protocols. Specialized bridges are available for converting Ethernet and token ring LANs.

**Bus:** A hardware device that connects internal hardware (e.g., CPU, printer control unit) or external hardware devices (e.g., stations in a network).

**Bus topology network:** A network topology in which all devices in a local area network (LAN) are attached to a line directly and all signals pass through each of the devices. Each device has a unique identity and can recognize the signals intended for it.

**Byte:** Eight bits that represent a character, such as a letter, symbol, or number.

**Cable modem:** A hardware device that sends and receives data over the cable television infrastructure. It is ideal for home use where fast access to the Internet is needed. A cable modem transmits data at a speed ranging from 500 Kbps to 2 Mbps, much faster than an ISDN line (from 128 Kbps to 1.54 Mbps) and a standard modem (28K to 56K).

**CD-ROM:** *See* compact disc read-only memory.

**Client:** *See* client/server.

**Client/server:** A computing architecture in which the client (any computer connected to a network, the user's computer) makes a service request from a server, which fulfills the request. A server is a computer station that stores the software that a client accesses.

**Coaxial cable:** A cable used to connect hardware devices in a LAN. It transmits data at a speed up to 500 Mbps (megabytes per second).

**Compact disc read-only memory (CD-ROM):** A read-only optical disc that stores a pre-recorded piece of software. A CD-ROM program cannot be altered or erased.

**Content designators:** The components of MARC 21 records, including the leader, fixed field, tags, indicators, subfield codes, and delimiters.

**Database:** A collection of data organized so that its contents can easily be accessed, managed, and updated.

**Digital Subscriber Line (DSL):** A digital line that uses a standard twisted-pair cable. It has a higher transfer rate than an ISDN line.

**DOS:** Disk operating system; it is character-based.

**DSL:** *See* Digital Subscriber Line.

**Dublin Core:** A standard that consists of fifteen elements for cataloging Internet resources.

**Dumb barcodes:** Barcodes that do not identify any items until they are linked to these items in the online system. Dumb barcodes usually have the name of a media center or library but not the author, title, or call number of an item.

**E-1 line:** A European digital transmission format and the equivalent of the North American T-carrier system.

**Ethernet:** One of the oldest and most widely used network architecture. It is based on the Institute of Electrical and Electronics Engineers (IEEE) Carrier-Sense Multiple Access/Collision Detection (CSMA/CD) 802.3 standard, an access-control technique that attempts to detect and recover from collisions.

**eXtensible Markup Language (XML):** A coding language for the Web that describes the content of a Web page in terms of what data are being described rather than in terms of how they are displayed. This language is ideal for coding MARC records for the Web due to its flexibility.

**Fast Ethernet:** A network architecture that transmits data at 100 Mbps, a much faster rate than Ethernet.

**FDDI:** *See* Fiber distributed data interface.

**Fiber distributed data interface (FDDI):** A network architecture that uses a token-passing technology. It runs at 100 Mbps (10 times as fast as Ethernet and about twice as fast as a T-3 carrier line). It can extend up to sixty miles in distance.

**Fiber optic cable:** A small, lightweight cable with a large bandwidth. It has a transmission speed of more than 2 Gbps (Giga bits per second) and a signal attenuation of more than sixty kilometers.

**File server:** One of the servers in a client/server network. Other servers that may exist in this network are Web servers, mail servers, and database servers.

**File transfer protocol (FTP):** A standard for exchanging and downloading files over the Internet.

**Frame relay:** A packet-switching protocol for connecting devices on a Wide Area Network (WAN) at speeds up to 45 Mbps.

**FTP:** *See* File transfer protocol.

**Gateway:** A hardware device that performs protocol conversion between different types of networks or applications (e.g., TCP/IP to Netware IPX/SPX and vice versa).

**Gigabyte:** One billion bytes.

**Graphical User Interface (GUI):** Software that allows users to interface with software through the use of icons, graphics, and textual information. This contrasts with character- or text-based interfaces (e.g., DOS, Lynx).

**GUI:** *See* Graphical User Interface.

**Home page:** The first screen one sees when connecting to a site on the World Wide Web.

**HTML:** *See* Hypertext Markup Language.

**Http:** *See* Hypertext Transfer Protocol.

**Hub:** A hardware device that joins computer communication lines that are together in a star topology network.

**Hypertext Markup Language (HTML):** A code used to write hypertext documents for the World Wide Web.

**Hypertext Transfer Protocol (http):** A standard used for accessing sites, particularly World Wide Web sites, on the Internet. The abbreviation http appears at the beginning of a site address.

**Hytelnet:** A tool for accessing resources via Telnet on the Internet.

**Infrared technology (IR):** A type of wireless LAN that uses the invisible part of light to carry data. It is usually limited to short distances because infrared cannot penetrate through opaque objects.

**Integrated Service Digital Network (ISDN):** A standard for transmitting information (data, voice, and video) over a digital communications line. This method of transmitting data is much faster than transmitting data over a traditional telephone line.

**Integrated software:** A software package with modules that work independently from each other and concurrently with one another.

**Interface:** A set of operating system commands, display formats, and other devices provided by a computer or a program to allow a user to communicate and use the computer or program.

**Internet:** A worldwide system of computer networks; a network of networks.

**Intranet:** A private network within an institution. The main purpose of an intranet is to share an institution's information and computing resources. An intranet may look like a private version of the Internet. It may be lined to the Internet using one or more gateways.

**IP:** *See* Transmission Control Protocol/Internet Protocol.

**IPAC** (Internet public access catalog): A public access catalog available on the Internet/Web. This term is not commonly used. The most commonly used terms are Web PAC and Web OPAC.

**IPX/SPX: Internetwork Packet Exchange/Sequenced Package Exchange.** A networking protocol from Novell that interconnects networks that use Novell's Netware clients and servers. IPX manages the forwarding of packets in the network; SPX handles packet sequencing.

**ISDN:** *See* Integrated Service Digital Network.

**Java:** An object-oriented programming language designed for use on the Internet/Web.

**Jazz drive:** A portable hard disk drive that is used for backing up files and for archival purposes. It can store 1 to 2 gigabyte of data, depending on the type.

**LAN:** *See* Local area network.

**LM_NET:** An Internet listserv for media specialists and librarians.

**Local area network (LAN):** A set of interconnected hardware devices designed to share software and hardware peripherals. A LAN is usually confined to a fairly small geographical area, one building, or a group of buildings close to each other. LANs can be bridged to communicate with one another.

**Mainframe computer:** A large computer, typically manufactured by a large company such as IBM, for large-scale computing purposes. Historically, a mainframe is associated with centralized rather than distributed computing.

**MAN:** *See* Metropolitan area network.

**MARC:** Machine-readable cataloging. It is a bibliographic standard that was developed by the Library of Congress.

**MARC 21, MARC for the twenty-first century:** The latest MARC bibliographic standard that combines U.S. MARC and Canadian MARC standards.

**MAU:** *See* Multiple Access Unit.

**Megabyte:** One million bytes.

**MegaHertz (mHz):** One million cycles per second. A unit of measurement used to indicate the clock speed of a computer microprocessor.

**Metropolitan area network (MAN):** A network that serves as a backbone to connect LANs in a city or region. It uses fiber optics, leased telephone lines (e.g., T-1, T-3), radio, or infrared transmission devices to connect LANs to a WAN.

**MHz:** *See* MegaHertz.

**Microcomputer Library Interchange Format (MicroLIF):** A standard established in 1987 by a group of library vendors to allow the exchange of MARC records in microcomputer-based automated systems. In 1991, this standard became know as U.S. MARC/MicroLIF Protocol for its conformity with the Library of Congress U.S. MARC. *See also* U.S. MARC/MicroLIF Protocol.

**MicroLIF:** *See* Microcomputer Library Interchange Format.

**Miniframe computer:** A scaled-down mainframe computer. The lines between miniframe and mainframe computers have blurred in the last few years, as minicomputers have become as powerful as mainframe computers.

**Module:** A component of a software program that represents a function and performs tasks associated with it.

**Multiple Access Unit (MAU):** A hub that is used in a ring topology network.

**Nesting:** A process of using parentheses around search statements when more than one Boolean operator exists. It is also referred to as nested logic. It is mainly used to instruct database retrieval software to follow the appropriate order of processing of Boolean operators.

**Network:** A series of points or nodes interconnected by communication paths. Networks can interconnect with other networks and may contain subnetworks.

**Novell Netware:** An IBM-compatible network operating system.

**OCLC:** *See* Online Computer Library Center

**Online Computer Library Center:** A nationwide bibliographic utility that enables resource sharing among libraries and other member institutions.

**Online public access catalog (OPAC):** An automation software module that is used by patrons to find and retrieve information. In a non-automated environment, the card catalog serves this purpose.

**OPAC:** *See* Online public access catalog.

**Operating system:** A computer program that monitors, supervises, and executes functions in a computer.

**PAC (public access catalog):** See Online public access catalog.

**Peer-to-peer network:** A network in which computers are connected to one another to share software (e.g., automation programs) and hardware (e.g., printers) without the use of a dedicated server.

**Platform:** In computers, a platform is an underlying computer system on which application programs can run. On personal computers, Windows 2000 and the Macintosh are examples of platforms.

*Precision One:* A CD-ROM database of MARC records developed by Brodart Automation Company. It is mainly used for retrospective conversion.

**PRI:** *See* Primary Rate Interface.

**Primary Rate Interface (PRI):** One of the levels of service provided by an ISDN supplier. It consists of twenty-three B-channels and one 64 Kpbs D-channel using a T-1 line or 30 B-channels and 1 D-channel using an E1 line. Thus, a Primary Rate Interface user on a T-1 line can have up to 1.544 MBPS service or up to 2.048 Mbps service on an E1 line.

**Protocol:** A set of rules that describes how to transmit data across a network.

**Read-only memory:** A permanent memory that cannot be changed.

**Recon:** *See* Retrospective conversion.

**Repeater:** A hardware device used to connect one or more segments of a cable to re-amplify the signal received on one segment before it reaches the next segment, thus increasing the attenuation signal.

**Request for proposal (RFP):** A document that includes essential and preferred functional specifications for an integrated online automation system.

**Retrospective conversion:** The process of converting a library's shelflist cards into a machine-readable format (i.e., U.S. MARC) that can be stored and retrieved by automation software.

**RFP:** *See* Request for proposal.

**Ring topology network:** A topology in which computers in a local area network (LAN) are attached to repeaters connected in a closed loop. Data are transmitted in one direction around the ring and can be read by all attached computers.

**ROM:** *See* Read-only memory.

**Router:** A hardware device that is used to forward data from one LAN to another or from a WAN to another.

**School Interoperability Framework (SIF):** A software package that allows the integration of student information into an automated library system. SIF is a new trend for school libraries.

**Server:** A computer station that stores the software that a client accesses. See also Client/server.

**Shelflist:** A section of a card catalog that contains a master copy of each cataloged item in a library's collection. Shelflist cards are usually filed by call number (e.g., Dewey Decimal, Library of Congress).

**Shielded twisted-pair (STP):** A bulky, heavy weight wire that provides excellent protection against electromagnetic interference and crosstalk among wires.

**SIF:** *See* School Interoperability Framework.

**Smart barcodes:** Barcodes that are linked to their respective items during retrospective conversion. Each smart barcode has the title, author, and call number of its respective item and the name of the library.

**Stand-alone software:** Non-integrated software with modules that work independently of each other. Each module is booted individually for access.

**Star topology network:** A topology in which each device in a local area network (LAN) is directly connected to a common central node, usually via two point-to-point links, one for transmission and one for reception.

**STP:** *See* Shielded twisted-pair.

**T-carrier system:** A digital telephone system, such as T-1 line, which carries twenty-four separate channels at a transmission rate of 64 Kbps. each for a total transmission rate of 1.54 Mbps.

**TCP/IP:** *See* Transmission Control Protocol/Internet Protocol.

**Telnet:** A software program that allows remote login on the Internet.

**Thin client:** In a client/server network architecture, a thin client is software designed to require low system resources by relying on the server for the majority of data processing tasks.

**Token ring:** A network architecture that uses a token-passing technology, which allows frames of data to be attached to the token.

**Token ring network:** A local area network (LAN) in which all computers are connected in a ring or star topology and a token-passing scheme is used to prevent the collision of data between two computers that want to send messages at the same time.

**Topology:** The physical layout or structure consisting of paths and switches that provide the communications interconnection among nodes of a network.

**Transmission Control Protocol/Internet Protocol (TCP/IP):** A set of two protocols used for all communications over the Internet.

**Turnkey system:** An automated library system with software and hardware preconfigured by an automation vendor. It is a "ready to go" system.

**Twisted-pair cable:** A copper wire that connects home and many business computers to a telephone company.

**Unicode:** A system for the interchange, processing, and display of the written texts of diverse languages.

**Uniform Resource Locator (URL):** A standard for specifying addresses for sites on the World Wide Web.

**Uninterruptible power supply (UPS):** A hardware device that keeps a file server running for a short time after a power shortage.

**Union catalog:** An online catalog that combines more than one library collection. A user can search for an item in a single library catalog or in all libraries' catalogs simultaneously.

**United States Machine-Readable Cataloging (U.S. MARC):** A bibliographic standard for cataloging materials in automated systems. It allows the interchange of bibliographic information across automated systems. It is used and distributed by the Library of Congress. The latest standard is MARC 21.

**UNIX:** An interactive timesharing operating system. It is a trademark of AT&T Bell Laboratories. It runs on minicomputers and powerful microcomputers.

**Unshielded twisted-pair (UTP):** One of the most common kinds of copper telephone wiring. UTP is a small, lightweight cable used in telephone connections and most LANs. It is inexpensive and relatively easy to install, but it is susceptible to data loss due to electromagnetic interference and crosstalk among wires.

**URL:** *See* Uniform Resource Locator.

**U.S. MARC:** *See* United States Machine-Readable Cataloging.

**U.S. MARC/MicroLIF Protocol:** A 1991 update to the standard MicroLIF. It is fully compatible with Library of Congress U.S. MARC. The latest standard is MARC 21.

**UTP:** *See* Unshielded twisted-pair.

**WAN:** *See* Wide area network.

**Web OPAC:** An online public access catalog available on the Web.

**Web PAC:** A public access catalog available on the Web. It is the same as Web OPAC and IPAC.

**Wide area network (WAN):** A statewide, regional, nationwide, or worldwide network, for example, OCLC and the Internet.

**Wireless LAN:** A LAN that is not based on cables or wires for connecting hardware devices. Wireless LANs use infrared technology or radio frequency. They require access points and adapters to operate.

**WLAN:** See Wireless LAN.

**World Wide Web (WWW):** An Internet server that combines text, images, audio, and video and is based on hypertext. A Web browser is required to view and use the Web in a graphical format.

**WWW:** *See* World Wide Web.

**XML:** *See* eXtensible Markup Language.

**Z39.50:** A standard that allows various computer systems to execute, search, retrieve, and display information in one common interface format, regardless of the hardware, software, database structure, or platform used. This standard is being implemented in many OPACs to facilitate their access on the World Wide Web.

**Zip drive:** A small, portable disk drive used primarily for backing up and archiving personal computer files. It can hold 100 or 250 megabytes of data, depending on the type.

# Index